Falling Out of Stride

What Comes Next Book One

Katharine E. Smith

HEDDON PUBLISHING

www.heddonpublishing.com
www.facebook.com/heddonpublishing
@PublishHeddon

Katharine E. Smith is an independent author of contemporary and literary fiction, including the bestselling Coming Back to Cornwall series.

Falling Out of Stride is the first full-length book of the What Comes Next series, which is preceded by *First Christmas*, a novella set at the beautiful Soulton Long Barrow.

A Philosophy graduate, Katharine initially worked in the IT and charity sectors. She turned to freelance editing in 2009, which led to her setting up Heddon Publishing, working with independent authors across the globe.

Katharine lives in Shropshire, UK, with her husband, their two children, and two excitable dogs.

You can find details of her books on her website:

www.katharineesmith.com

Information about her work with other authors can be found here:

www.heddonpublishing.com

and

www.heddonbooks.com

For Dad xx

Beginnings

It begins with a kiss, as so many stories do. Although… is the kiss really the beginning? I have seen this coming for a while, but been powerless to stop it. And besides, where does any story really start? We could move back and forth in anyone's life – to before they are born, even – to find what we might call a beginning; the event or events which set something in motion, and there will always be something else before that. Cause and effect to infinity.

But I am going off-topic, and I've only just begun (don't even think about it).

Back to the kiss, and the beginning of this particular part of our story…

It's New Year's Eve and my family have all come home to roost – not an uncommon situation, except that this year somebody is missing. Somebody vital. That somebody is me. It is a handful of months since I died, and my family are still living in that aching space where disbelief, anger, shock, and unbearable sadness ebb and flow, sometimes all of them washing in to shore together.

My husband and children, my son-in-law and my dog, have all gathered at the family home, and tonight they're in the living room, which I once spent a long weekend decorating, in Graham's absence; ostensibly to surprise him but actually to avoid him querying my choice of colours (dove grey and sage if you're interested) before he'd had a chance to see them for himself. I knew it would look wonderful – soothing and calm – but Graham wouldn't have been able to imagine it. "Won't it just look cold?" he would have asked. And I'd have felt guilty, imposing my tastes on what was a room that we shared, even though otherwise we would almost inevitably have ended up with Graham's choice of colours instead. He'd have gone for the same colour on all four walls – something neutral – complemented by a white ceiling. And this would have looked nice, but I had wanted something a little bit different. And I had loved seeing the room transform, removing all traces of the floral wallpaper which had adorned it since before we moved in.

What with the children, and work, and various other life events, we had just never got round to redecorating, although we had talked about it often enough. That weekend, I worked day and night in Graham's absence, creating this soft, gentle space, which made me think of being in the clouds. It sounds stupid, I know, but that's how it made me feel.

Besides, the decorating itself gave me something to do; a focus, helping to stave off 'empty nest syndrome'. It was not all that long since Tom had gone, and years since Annie had left for uni, Kitty following shortly afterwards. I missed them, and the often longed-for time to myself was not necessarily all I had expected it to be.

Graham was away with his childhood friends; usually pretty poor at the social-life side of things, he has against all odds remained a part of his school-days friendship group and even all these years later they get together for an annual weekend away – sailing, or walking, or just pubbing (depending on the state of everyone's health). To be fair, he had asked me along too but by that point in our life together I no longer felt the need to fit in with his old pals. When Graham returned, I led him through to see the fruits of my labour and he was visibly shocked; initially, perhaps, a little annoyed that I'd made this major change without his involvement, but he'd clearly had a good time with his friends and was feeling generous. Almost. "Well, I do wish we'd discussed it-" he couldn't find it in himself to be 100% giving - "this is my room too, after all, but… I do like it. It's actually quite relaxing."

I'd smiled to myself, and a tiny little internal cheer went up because I had won this small battle, and I'd pushed something through for once. I'd encouraged him to sit down and enjoy the new room, while I made us both a cup of tea.

Now, the décor is the last thing on anyone's mind – except perhaps Kitty's, as that's how her mind works. She thinks in colours, and shapes. It's like seeing everything through a filter, and I think my colour scheme is helping her now. I hope it is, she needs to calm down. She needs to breathe. Thankfully, faithful Mavis, my soft, cuddly spaniel, is burrowed into her side, offering physical comfort and warmth. While Kitty strokes Mavis, her heartbeat slows ever-so-slightly but still, her mind is in turmoil, spinning from recent events. She's contemplating 'this time last year'; a train of thought that they all find themselves stuck on very regularly. She is also watching her brother-in-law try unsuccessfully to secure his wife's attention, and approval.

Alex is flicking through the channels on the TV, talking to Annie about their first New Year's Eve together. Trying to remind her of the effort he'd put into that evening: the candle-lit dinner at a posh Shrewsbury restaurant, for which he had saved up for weeks in order to treat her; the walk along the riverside, timed to perfection so that they reached the church just as the bells were ringing in the new year; a kiss, which Alex has never forgotten, although he wonders sometimes if Annie has; and finally a night in a hotel, rather than trying to squeeze onto the last train home and have the magic of the evening rubbed away by New Year's drunkards.

"Remember, Annie?" Alex asks. "That was the best night of my life."

Annie just smiles, absentmindedly. Alex reads this as her not caring. Kitty thinks the same. Only I know that Annie's mind is not focused on her husband or his words and sentimental memories, and not because she doesn't care – although she does wish he would shut up, and just give her a chance to process her own quiet thoughts – but because she is trying her utmost to hold it together, as she has been ever since I died. Ever since I became ill, in fact, and went to her house to tell her the news, one evening, when Alex was out. She had held it together then, and so had I – being strong for each other – but when I'd left we had both let our tears spill, on our own. Me in my car, she in their bedroom, falling onto the duvet and pushing her face into the pillow as she had done during so many teenage meltdowns. Only this time she wasn't saying: "I hate her." She was pleading, "Don't take her." To whom she was addressing this plea, she wasn't sure. Anyone who would listen, I suppose.

The problem now is that Annie is distancing herself from her husband, and he's feeling it. He misses me too, he has found; after all, they have been together a long time, and I've been a large part of his life. A second mother to him at times. Alex is sad as well and I do know that he is allowed to be. He made the mistake of telling Annie once, though, and felt the full weight of her fury.

"How do you think I feel?" she had shouted at him, her face red and her energy raw. It was unfair, as many of her criticisms of him are. And, as often happens, she realised this when she had time to think about it, but she did not know how to tell him. And

5

besides, despite her guilt, she did not want to tell him.

So Kitty sits quietly, watchfully, on the outside the picture of calm while within she is panicking. Feeling things falling apart. Annoyed at her sister that she doesn't see how lucky she is to have Alex. How Kitty would have loved Olly to have been as attentive to her. Yes, Alex can be a little irritating – and she'd quite like to snatch the TV remote off him to stop him channel-hopping. She'd like to turn the TV off altogether, in fact. But lately she's felt like she and Alex have made a connection; it's not very nice, she knows, but it's like they're bonding through Annie's coldness. She smiles at Alex now, and he smiles back then looks quickly at Annie, but Kitty sees he glances straight back at her.

Oh Kitty, I think, but I am powerless. All I can do is watch.

I turn my attention from my daughters to my husband. Graham has given himself a job, as he has found this an effective way of getting through the days. Even when I was still alive, but ill, he realised that being useful was the thing that could save him. I may have given him a helping hand with this. I would ask him to fetch me things, even if I knew I'd have been able to get them myself. Or I'd issue instructions for shopping and cooking and washing.

Somewhere along the line in our life together, although both Graham and I worked full-time, those responsibilities had fallen largely to me. It was just easier, and quicker, if I did them, I would tell myself, although I was damned if the same fate would befall my girls.

There had been a spell after Tom was born, when I was too ill to perform all these tasks, and Graham had picked up the mantel. He had been guilt-ridden, too, after an ill-advised affair with his secretary, but as my health returned and his guilt became less immediate, somehow our domestic life regained its previous status quo.

Then, ill once again, once Graham got into the swing of it he remembered he could do all of these things, and more. And I knew he would be OK. Not happy, or not for a long time yet, but OK.

It's been harder than ever for my husband this last week, between Christmas and New Year; that unique time when everything seems to grind to a halt – except for retail sales and pantomimes, or heavy drinking, none of which Graham would want to indulge in during normal times, and this is far from a normal time. His job tonight is keeping the fire going, keeping everyone warm, and he is attentive to a fault. So much so that he's nominated Tom to keep the drinks and snacks flowing, having learned long ago that both our girls would castigate him if he asked them to take on this task. "Don't be so sexist, Dad!" either Annie or Kitty would cry, and he'd back away, slightly nervously. Tom, meanwhile, would gamely take on whatever was required. It's been good for him, growing up with two strong older sisters. He's got a good take on women, although he has avoided anything like a serious relationship so far. Maybe he's got too good a take on women. Perhaps he doesn't want the bother.

So Tom is back and forth between the lounge and the kitchen, and the garden, where he has been smoking a couple of sneaky joints. He thinks he masks the smell by staying out in the cold air for a while afterwards but Kitty is well aware of it, and it crosses Annie's mind, too, although somewhere near the back of it, drifting like Tom's smoke amidst the mess of other thoughts. Tom is also fielding messages from Amy, a girl he met at college, who is trying her best to be a shoulder for him to cry on, in the hope it will lay the ground for something more. But Tom can see through this. He is kind and respectful in his replies, but he makes sure not to be too quick to respond, and he keeps his answers nondescript and non-committal. He goes up to his room every now and then as well, to 'build' his joints as he calls it (oh the things I know about him now, that I never did before!), and again to look for a book he can't remember the name of. By flitting about here, there and everywhere, he is managing to some extent to avoid the weight of my absence. And somehow, the evening passes.

Alex continues doing his best to be attentive to Annie. He checks if she is alright for a drink... does she want something to eat? Is she tired? They don't have to stay up until midnight if she doesn't want to.

Graham keeps his eyes on the fire, although the girls – particularly Kitty – try to draw him in to conversation. He is oblivious to the situation playing out in the very same room he is in. Annie's irritation, crackling like the fire. Alex, panicking at his wife's apparent rejection of him, finding his eyes drawn to kind, receptive Kitty.

I want Alex to stop drinking, and to look at his wife, my oldest child, and see her properly. To understand what she actually needs. Yes, she is a pain in the arse sometimes, and she is too harsh to him, but it's like he's grown up with a set idea of what a relationship should be like, and he won't budge from it.

He wants to hold hands with Annie, but she's not that type. He wants her to be happy to see him when he gets home from work, and for her to miss him when they're apart. Again, she is not that type. He wants to provide and care for Annie; he wants her to lean on him, but he never stops long enough for her to give it a try.

It's like they're misfiring all the time. Because as much as I wish Alex would see Annie properly, I also wish she would see what she is doing to him. He's not grown-up yet; an adult, yes, but not a grown-up, although he wants to be. And her attitude only makes him more vulnerable; a lost little boy wanting very much to be – and to be seen to be – a man.

From my new vantage point, I can see that, despite

everything, Annie does love Alex, but perhaps not in the way that he would like. She, being Annie, thinks he should be striving to be the best he can be. But she's not shy with her criticism and of course it makes him feel unloved, and over the years they've got themselves stuck in this stupid situation where they don't communicate their feelings and then Alex does something stupid, as he is doing now; becoming increasingly drunk and increasingly irritating, although he's trying to be charming.

I can see it all playing out before me.

And then there's Kitty – *oh, Kitty* – feeling sorry for Alex. She likes him. She sees the good in him (and there really is a lot of good in my son-in-law, despite his faults), and she knows what hard work her older sister can be. Kitty is thinking again that Annie doesn't know how lucky she is. Annie has no idea what it's like to have her heart broken.

Kitty, I want to say, *it's not all about relationships*. Except that at her age, it almost always is.

And this is a learning experience for me; that I cannot fix what is going on. I can only watch, and wait, and hope that they make it right. All of them.

It's difficult, and frustrating, but somewhere inside me there is also perhaps a very slight sense of relief, that this is not, and can't be, my responsibility.

At around half past eleven, Kitty yawns. Mavis looks up at her, and Kitty smiles and ruffles the dog's long ears. "Want to sleep in with me tonight, Maeve?" she whispers.

"You're not going to bed, are you?" Alex asks. "Come on, you've nearly made it to midnight. Stay up and see the new year in. Watch the fireworks."

"Maybe she doesn't want to," Annie says bluntly.

"You do, don't you Kitty?" Alex asks, doubtfully.

"Well…"

"It's our first year without Mum, isn't it?" Annie says, exasperated. "What is there to look forward to?"

And Kitty feels a lurching in her stomach as Annie has just thoughtlessly scattered a handful of words which express exactly what she is thinking, and feeling. She's scared, to step into the next year, and even further away from me.

Our first year without Mum. Kitty knows that it's silly to think like this. It's just another day. But we humans create this all for ourselves, don't we? The milestones, the celebrations, the anniversaries. Fantastic and celebratory on the way up. Miserable and agonising on the way back down.

"I'll stay up," Kitty says with a small smile.

"Great," says Alex. "I'll get the champagne."

Annie rolls her eyes.

As five to midnight rolls around, Alex starts polishing the glasses. "Will you have one, Graham?" he asks kindly, seeing his father-in-law gazing mindlessly into the flames.

"What's that?" Graham turns, blinking into the room, almost surprised to find his family still there with him. "Oh yes, thank you, Alex."

And Alex pops the cork, fills the glasses, makes everybody stand for the countdown, although nobody else feels like it.

"Five... four... three... two... one!" Alex announces as Big Ben tolls on the TV and the annual extravagance of fireworks begins. Mavis, never a fan of fireworks, runs from the room and Kitty follows her. Alex goes to kiss Annie on the lips but Annie turns her head so he gets her cheek instead. Tom hugs Graham, then Graham hugs Annie, while Tom and Alex shake hands.

"Where's Kitty?" Alex asks, his cheeks flushed from his wife's rebuttal.

"She went after Mavis, I think... bloody fireworks," says Tom, flopping down onto the settee and downing half his glass of champagne.

"Steady on," Graham murmurs, putting his own glass – barely touched – on the mantelpiece.

"I'll go and see if she's OK... shall I?" Alex turns to Annie. She just shrugs.

Further evidence of her ambivalence to him, Alex thinks, but I know this is not about him. This is about the churning inside of Annie. At memories of New Years past, and that thought which she had vocalised, that she is embarking on her first ever year without me by her side.

The only one who really knew me, she thinks now, miserably. And she's half-right. Graham understands Professional Annie. They share skills and knowledge, and a way of thinking that is alien to me. But I do know her. I know her struggles and her awkwardness, and how much she longs to be different to how she is; how much she longs to be the same as everyone else. To be as easy in company as Kitty and Tom are. To make people laugh, not make them shuffle uncomfortably as sometimes happens if she tries to make a joke in a work meeting. All of this passes above Alex's head, though.

He moves into the cool hallway, noting the pile of Christmas cards on the table there. I would normally have these Blu-tacked all along the banister, up the stairs, on the backs of doors... This Christmas, Graham couldn't bring himself to. It was as much as he could do to put up the tree, and that was only at Tom's insistence. When Kitty had arrived home, she'd dug out some of the other decorations, stringing up the lights along the banisters, and around the windows. Adorning the pictures with tinsel garlands, like I used to do. All these little things the living do to try and keep some kind of contact with the dead. Wearing our jumpers, cardigans; our scarves, our jewellery. Listening to the music we loved; reading the books we left on our bedside tables. It is not futile, as deep down they suspect it might be. It's beautiful, and it works.

"Kitty?" Alex calls softly. He hears her voice upstairs, and follows the sound, up to her childhood bedroom.

"Knock, knock," he says, because her door is open.

"Hi Alex," she replies. "I'm just keeping Maeve company."

"Poor thing," he says. He doesn't know if he means Mavis or Kitty. "Can I come in?"

"Sure."

The room is in darkness, but Kitty is just visible on the bed. She sits up, keeping one hand on my beautiful dog, who is still trembling. Kitty hopes that there will be no more fireworks tonight. She feels exhausted from the effort of the last year, and she still can't shake that 'this time last year' feeling. She had been out in the pub with her school friends, Olly having opted to spend Christmas and New Year with his parents. She didn't get in till three am. She remembers feeling free and happy, and trying to bury that half-thought that maybe Olly was not the man for her. Perhaps he was not the man she'd thought he was. She had not wanted to acknowledge it.

"Happy new year," Alex ventures now. He feels a little light-headed and out of his depth, but at the same time somehow more sure of himself than he has been in years.

"Happy new year," Kitty replies, feeling the emptiness of the words but nevertheless grateful that Alex has come to see her.

He sits next to her, to give her a hug, and finds himself holding her tight, all of his loneliness squashed between them. Something clicks somewhere in the darkness, on this night which barely feels real, and although he pulls away, their faces move forwards, eyes searching for the other's in the dim light. Their lips meet, just for a moment, but that moment is enough. Alex closes his eyes. It feels like swimming underwater. He wants to dive further, but Kitty pulls back sharply, in shock.

"Alex?" they hear Annie's voice from the stairwell. "I'm going to bed."

And suddenly everything seems incredibly real.

1

So really you could find any number of beginnings to this story, but let's stick with that kiss – between a man and his wife's sister. Boiled down to those bare bones, it sounds horribly sordid, and I suppose in a way it is, but firstly it involves my wonderfully kind, sensitive and thoughtful younger daughter. I know she is not perfect, but I would never think of her as sordid. Secondly, as with so much in life (and death), there are many sides to this story. A failed relationship. A sad relationship. Bereavement. Grief. Loneliness. Rejection. Dejection. Alcohol.

But the booze is not to blame. This has been brewing a while now, this thing between Alex and Kitty. It only really clicked for me when they were all here at the long barrow together, on Christmas Day. I saw it clearly then but there had been clues before. Even at my funeral, though I don't think either of them were consciously aware of it, when Annie wouldn't let Alex hold her hand, and he'd turned instead to Kitty; put his arm around her. Wanting so much that role of protector. To be taken seriously.

He has never voiced it to anyone – I want to say 'not even Annie' but knowing what we know about their relationship, I don't think it's all that surprising – but Alex knows that people sometimes laugh at him behind his back. He's caught the odd smirking look exchanged between colleagues in meetings, when they think he's not looking. It hurts but he tries to push it aside. Tells himself that it doesn't matter, and that all that counts is his family.

The funeral presented him with the opportunity to present a different side of himself; which is not to say he didn't genuinely want to comfort and protect his wife – or failing that, her sister – but he was also pleased to have the chance to be seen to be doing so.

Kitty, whose supposed 'partner' Olly had let her down; told her he couldn't come, because he was needed for a work meeting (the final nail in the coffin, if you'll pardon my pun), was grateful then to Alex. He offered her a solidity; somebody to lean against, while her world was falling apart. She read a poem – *The Dash* – and before she went up to the lectern, Alex had squeezed her arm. While she walked back, quickly, not wanting to be watched, she looked to him and saw him smile at her.

She knew – she knows – it is wrong, but her head is a mess. It's hard to think clearly when you're drowning in grief. I remember that from when my own parents died. And Judy, too, my sister and my greatest friend. I don't suppose it was any coincidence that when Nick came into my life, not all that long after her death, I didn't want to let him go.

Kitty lay awake all night, fretting about what had happened. In the morning, while the world was still in darkness, she was sitting up, jotting a note to them all, apologising, saying she had to go back home, to work; Meg was ill. It was a lie, but nobody would know. She felt particularly guilty towards Graham, knowing that he would be waking up to face the new year on his own, but it couldn't be helped. There was no way she could face Annie, or Alex. Or Tom. Would he know? Would he guess? She couldn't think how, but then it felt like the guilt was oozing out of her, and she wouldn't be able to hide it.

Besides, she reasoned, she had been there for the main days over Christmas, and she'd spent lots of time with her dad. Now she needed time, and space, to think. It was important to be selfish sometimes, she told herself. That was what Meg had told her; Meg, the manager of the kennels where Kitty works, whose life revolves almost entirely around all the dogs. Like Kitty, she too had been let down by a boyfriend. In fact, he had treated her so badly that she had resolved never to have a relationship again. He had not liked Bovril, the dog she had back then; he'd thought that she gave too much of herself to 'that bloody animal', so when she'd finally kicked the boyfriend out, she decided that to spite him she would fill her life with even more.

Meg is ten years older than Kitty and she lives very much hand to mouth, but she always makes sure she can pay her staff, and she always finds a way to feed those dogs and cover vet bills, and heat the kennels. Kitty knows Meg sometimes sleeps in the office in the kennel building, saving on heating her own ramshackle house. She found her there one morning, hurriedly shoving a sleeping bag into its case.

"Meg…" Kitty had said.

"What?" Meg's face was a mixture of obstinacy and embarrassment.

"Please don't tell me you've been here all night."

"Uh, it got late, and I couldn't face the cold walk back to the house."

"I don't believe you."

"Believe what you like."

"Meg, you can come and crash at my place, you know. It's easier now Olly's gone."

"I can't leave the dogs, can I?"

"Of course you can't. Sorry. Well, I can stay over here sometimes, and you can have a proper night's sleep at my flat. A long, relaxing bath."

"Are you saying I smell?"

"Of course not." The fact is, though, she does. Just a bit. It's inevitable really, I suppose, spending so much time at that place. But it's not a horrible smell. Meg doesn't smell like an actual dog. It's almost chemical; clinical, from the regular cleaning of the kennels and walkways. Kitty continued, "But everyone deserves some time off, Meg. You more than most."

"You've got enough going on, Kitty. Don't worry about me. Just look out for yourself. Thank you, though." Meg's face had softened. "And you won't…?"

"Tell anyone you're dossing down here? No of course I won't." Kitty had put her arm around her boss, her mind filling with ideas for fundraisers. She imagined the team from *DIY SOS* coming to help out; Meg deserved something like that.

"Thank you, Kitty. You're a real friend."

Mavis, who had sneaked into Graham's room during the small hours of the morning, taking her place on what used to be my side of the bed, heard Kitty on the stairs, and came to the hallway to greet her.

"Go back to bed, Maeve," Kitty said, burrowing her face in the dog's soft fur. Mavis licked her ear then did as she was told, and slipped back into my old bedroom, curling up by Graham.

Does Mavis wonder where I am? When I'm coming back? Those first few weeks, she would look for me, but she doesn't anymore. I know she is almost aware of me sometimes; just a lift of her nose to the air, an interested wrinkle of her soft muzzle, tells me she catches some sense of something familiar, and much-loved. But it doesn't seem to bother her as I thought it might.

Carrying her bag, Kitty had tiptoed down the stairs. She picked up the small pile of Christmas presents – books, chocolates and a scarf – from underneath the table, and slid them into a carrier bag. As she reached the kitchen, placing the note on the surface by the kettle – the place she knew Graham would head to as soon as he was downstairs – she felt distinctly unsettled. I tried so hard to make her feel my presence then; to let her know she was not as alone as she felt, but she was far too deep inside herself to notice. Instead, holding back the tears, she carefully and slowly unlocked the back door, stepping into a world still guarded by the moon, stars hole-punched into the sky. Kitty imagined them not as masses of gas but as little piercings through a next level of the universe – offering a tiny glimpse of a brighter place – and she hoped she would find me there one day.

She messaged Meg, to let her know what was happening – or part of it at least:

Hi, I know you'll be up soon. Say hello to the dogs from me. I hope you don't mind but I need to get away and I had to make an excuse so I said you were ill and need me at work. I'll let you know when I'm back, and I will come across if you do need me. I might as well make myself useful. X

The thought of work; that combination of the routine and the unexpected, was enticing. There was something about the physicality of it, along with the sheer love of the dogs – and sometimes the challenge of a new rescue animal to work with – which kept Kitty there. The pay is terrible – thankfully Graham is helping her on that score – and she isn't putting as much time into her art as she'd like, but after I died, as she returned to a world which was at once familiar and utterly strange, it was the kennels, and working with Meg, that kept her going.

With the message sent, Kitty quietly put her bags on her passenger seat and then slid into the driver's side. It would take a couple of hours to get to her flat, but first she had a visit to make.

She might have known that I was there with her all along, that she didn't have to walk across the fields in the dark, following the path to the long barrow just to find me. But both she and I knew that it would also do her good.

I join her as she crosses the road from the parking area, next to the grand old hall, its windows in darkness but its brickwork illuminated by the light bouncing off the moon. She steps onto the solid path, which skirts the edge of a field and bends to the right, bordered by a hedgerow that buzzes with life in the summer but right now is still and apparently dead to the world, although Kitty's keen ear catches the sound of a mouse scurrying somewhere at the bottom of it, scratching and rummaging in the dead leaves.

She sees the very first colours of dawn pressing gently into the sky, and she allows her feet to fall into a pleasing rhythm, which she counts out in her head as she walks. As she rounds the bend towards the barrow, she hears a wood pigeon's soft call from the oak tree near the pond. She slows a little, her steps more gently now, and her mind turns towards the long barrow, and what lies within. At the doorway, she stops. Steps into the shelter, considering that change in sound and light as she crosses the threshold. Pressing the now-familiar code into the lock, she moves smoothly inside, greeting us all with a soft "Hello." She switches on the torch function of her phone, looking for the book of matches which is usually tucked to the right of the doorway, and she moves across to my niche, where she lights the candle.

She stops, and nearly sobs, considering the image on the stained-glass door. A family. Our family. Two parents, three children, and a dog. A house. A heart-shaped sun radiating love. No brother-in-law complicating matters.

"Oh Mum," she says, and she half-collapses onto her knees, on the cold stone seat in front of the niche. "What have I done?"

To not be able to hold her in this moment is one of the most painful things I've experienced of late. She doesn't cry, though; she is in too much shock for that, and besides, she doesn't feel like she deserves her own tears. This is not a time for self-pity. But what a mess.

She feels like banging her head against the stone pillar which stands sentinel next to my niche and those above and below, which are currently empty.

Thankfully, she doesn't give in to this impulse to bang her head and instead she turns and sits, leaning against the pillar despite the cold, feeling drained and bewildered. She'd known, of course, that she and Alex had been showing a little bit of interest in each other – a bit more than was healthy or right for a brother- and sister-in-law. But she hadn't really taken it in very consciously. In fact, it had seemed a very safe option because of course nothing was going to happen between them, was it? Kitty had been lonely in the wake of her failed relationship and, she imagined correctly, Alex was probably a bit lonely in his marriage. They both loved Annie, and both suffered sometimes in her coldness, so to find comfort in each other seemed natural – but not to this extent. Not so that they had actually kissed.

Now, my take on these things is a little different. I get it; I understand how, especially with young relationships, where the physical side of things is so vital, that a kiss, or a fumble, or sleeping together, constitute cheating on somebody. But to my mind, and considering what I had with Nick, these physical acts are only a part of it. An affair – cheating on somebody – doesn't just boil down to the physical. Illicit conversations, texts, and emails – choosing to trust and confide in somebody over your partner (especially if you are divulging details of your relationship): aren't these things equally, if not more, a betrayal? Surely they are just as painful for the injured party as knowing your partner has weakly acted upon a physical attraction?

I have punished myself with these thoughts for years, knowing that aside from one kiss what Nick and I had may not have been considered an affair, but strongly aware that my feelings for him and the amount of time he occupied my thoughts – not to mention how much I came to trust and rely on him emotionally – were at least as much a betrayal of my relationship with Graham as his sordid, sweaty sexual affair with his secretary had been.

Life is complicated.

But none of that is going to help Kitty now. She is berating herself for what has occurred and gradually, first double-checking she really is alone in here (having no idea how heard she really is), in the darkness she begins to find her voice.

"Mum. I've been such an idiot. I've betrayed Annie, in the worst way. And I don't know what to do about it." She lets out a sob but then stops herself. Sits up straight. She does not deserve to cry. She begins again, her voice bouncing softly around the dusky space. "Mum… I've kissed Alex. My own brother-in-law! What the fuck was I thinking? Sorry for the swear, Mum –" that, at least, makes her smile, knowing I was not much one for swearing, then she lets it all out, a stream of consciousness really, and I'm glad she feels able to – "but I can't believe that happened. Or I can't believe I let that happen. I mean, really, *he* kissed *me*, I think. But I let him. What do I do now? Do I tell Annie? I can't! Can I?" With nobody to answer her, she shakes her head vehemently. Wipes her nose on the back of her hand. "I can't. But I can't face her either. Not now. I… I left a note, saying I've had to go back to work. I'm a coward. And it's not fair on anyone. I've just left Dad, and Tom. And little Mavis…" The thought of my dog is enough to set her off crying properly. "Oh Mum," she sobs. "Oh Mum."

And then she folds her arms, drops her chin to her chest. Wishes she was small enough to curl up on the seat, and sleep. Hibernate. Wake up to find everything right with the world. If only.

As I've sat next to my girl, and listened, the others have made themselves scarce, and I've appreciated it. That is a potential problem with this shared space, that we are privy to each other's family's and friends' thoughts and feelings, sometimes arguments, when they come to visit. It doesn't matter, really, but it feels intrusive, just as it can if I know too much of my children's lives. We may be beyond the grave and beyond acting on, or reacting to, anything we hear, but it still feels wrong. People deserve their privacy.

Now, though, I feel Teresa by my side, and Kiran.

"Alright?" Kiran asks me, softly.

"Yes. Well, no!" I laugh.

None of what Kitty has said is a shock to me, of course. I've seen it all play out before me, but nonetheless it is difficult to feel my daughter's pain.

"Mortals, eh?" Teresa says, hoping to alleviate my pain. Kiran gives her a look. "Sorry," Teresa says.

"No, it's fine, really. I just wish I could help her straighten her head. Make her see it's not the end of the world."

"It is a tricky one, though," Teresa says. "You must admit, it's a bit of a sticky wicket."

"It's not ideal, I'll say that."

"My girls are always falling out," Kiran says. "Sometimes over little things, sometimes bigger. They find a way to sort it out."

"But have any of them kissed one of the other's husbands?"

"No," she admits.

I lay my hand lightly on my daughter's bowed head. Kitty feels the hairs on the back of her neck prickling but she mistakes it for early morning cold. She pulls her arms more tightly around herself, and she stands up. Time to go. She might as well get to work; make her lie to her family half-true. Besides, she would like to see Meg, and make a confession to somebody who can talk back. It's done her good, opening up in this semi-darkness, where nobody can hear her, but if she keeps this to herself, she is going to go mad. Meg, she thinks, might berate her, but she knows she can trust her – to keep a secret, and to offer good advice.

Kitty lays her hand gently on the stained-glass door, stroking the glass figures with her fingers, then she says, "Happy new year, Mum," and at once feels stupid, but she gazes through the glass to the shape of the urn within the niche and then blows out the candle, shrouding herself in darkness.

The doorway is clear to see against the gloom and once she is outside, Kitty is surprised to see that the sky has already soaked up much of the daylight from beyond the horizon, banishing the stars. She thinks briefly of how she and I used to make French toast, and let the milky mixture saturate the slices of bread, before laying them in the hot pan until they turned golden and crisp. Her stomach rumbles. Maybe she'll stop to get some breakfast on her journey. Or perhaps she'll buy egg, milk and bread, if anywhere's open, and make brunch for herself and Meg.

Kitty peers back into the chamber, to double-check she's definitely extinguished the candle, and then she carefully locks up, stepping outside, into the day. She starts to make her way back around the barrow, towards the path. She stops.

"Bye, Mum," she says, and contemplates how this stupid, ridiculous situation she has got herself into had cut through her grief for a while. Now, it comes back, full force, and sits alongside her confusion and guilt. This is not the best start to a new year.

As she trudges along, back towards the car and back towards reality, she doesn't notice the two figures, or the dog, across the fields. Only one of them sees her and it's a good job, too. It's a miracle Mavis hasn't clocked Kitty, but not so surprising with Tom, whose mind is otherwise occupied, not only by the sight of the short-eared owl but by the person who has pointed it out to him.

Although Kitty had indeed been alone inside the barrow while she made her confession, our Cecily, wonderful guardian of the barrow and friend to all of those who reside here (and our families) had arrived not long after her and, hearing her voice – and catching just an earful of Kitty's words – had remained discreetly outside.

Just how much she heard, I do not know, but on seeing Tom and Mavis approaching across the fields in the dawning light, she'd realised that they needed to be kept away and, lifesaver that she is, she found the perfect way to avert that particular disaster.

2

Tom had woken early – disturbed by Kitty leaving the house but unaware that was what had woken him. She had done her utmost to be quiet, but he's not sleeping well, and he sensed something. There is some truth in him having a sixth sense, which he sometimes wonders about. This morning, he'd sensed a disturbance in the force (he'd be pleased to hear me using that expression, borrowed from the *Star Wars* films he loves so much).

He's done well, these last few months, to try and maintain his positivity. He is determined to be a realist, as he perceives me to have been, and to face the situation head-on. He is right, that I was – am – a realist, but he didn't see those times, of which there were many, when I crumbled. Found myself praying to a god I didn't really believe in, to save me. To make me one of those rare, miraculous cases who somehow rallies in the face of incurable illness and finds it is not as incurable as first thought. Nobody, not even Graham, saw me at these times, when I allowed myself to collapse on the bed, or dissolve in the shower, and let darkness and despair flood through me for a while.

I had found myself thinking of Nick, and longing to see him, to lean on him. He and I, with our medical backgrounds, we knew the score. But as soon as I realised the situation, and that I was not going to get better, I had cut things off with him. Anything else would not have been fair to any of us.

Meanwhile Tom, always observing, had seen only my stoicism, and resolved to be the same. This is a problem now, though he doesn't see it. He is becoming increasingly exhausted by this determination to be 'strong'. He isn't sleeping, and he doesn't know how to sit still. Hence on this early New Year's morning, he finds himself softly calling Mavis (unbeknown to him, only just settled again after greeting Kitty), grabbing her lead, and exiting through the back door. He does not pass the driveway, so he does not notice that Kitty's car has gone. He's full of nervous energy and he needs to walk it off. The destination seems obvious.

As he walks the quiet streets, Tom sees another dog-walker, and they – humans and canines – greet each other politely, but aside from this they do not see another soul.

As he scoots into the fields behind the cul-de-sacs which sprout off the main road, he is aware that his route to the long barrow may not be strictly allowed, but it saves walking along the dangerous, footpathless road, and he and Mavis are always respectful. Tom's way brings him towards the barrow from an alternative perspective to that of most visitors, and it also means that yet again he is unaware of Kitty's car.

His mind is elsewhere, anyway; focusing on the increasing volume and variety of birdsong, and the skein of geese that fly honking overhead, making Mavis spin with excitement. And then, as they approach the now familiar site of the long barrow mounds, he hears a voice, before he sees the figure.

"Hello!" she calls to him, and he smiles to see Cecily, the friend to all, who has 'come out of her shell' since she's been working at the long barrow – this, her parents agree, is one of the plus points of her latest baffling career choice. She is not full-time at the barrow, although she is here as much as she can be. Cecily is also a waitress, and a cleaner, and an aspiring writer. She makes very little money from all of these things, and she knows her mum and dad think she could be doing better. Using her degree. She trained as a teacher, after all. But they hope that she will come to her senses and return to that world one day. In the meantime, they have agreed to support her in all the ways they can, and they never – well, rarely, or at least as little as possible – mention that they had hoped her life would be different.

"Hi," he says, pleased to see her.

Tom likes this girl. He thinks that he and Cecily might have quite a lot in common.

"Are you on your way to the barrow?" She is grateful for the semi-darkness, disguising her blush. Where on earth else would he be heading?

"Yeah. Come to wish Mum a happy new year."

She smiles at him sympathetically. "It must be strange not having her around."

"It is. Mavis misses her too, don't you girl?" He ruffles the spaniel's head. Mavis, not always overly friendly with people outside the family, regards Cecily, then trots up to her and sniffs her hand.

"Hello Mavis," Cecily smiles. "She's lovely," she says to Tom.

"She is. She was always Mum's dog really, she's not quite sure where she fits now."

"You seem to look after her well, though."

"She's my mate. My walking companion. I have to get out, every day if I can. It helps clear my head… walking, wildlife…" His voice trails off, self-conscious.

"I know exactly what you mean. Maybe I should get a dog."

"You should!" Tom enthuses. "Honestly, you won't regret it."

Cecily wonders if Kitty is still in the barrow. She can't turn and look and risk drawing Tom's attention that way. "Are you keen on birds?" she asks and again she blushes, thinking what a bad choice of words.

Tom just laughs. "Yes!" he grins. "Love them."

"Well, I know where we might see a short-eared owl, if you're interested. I saw one the other day, and I think I know where it's nesting. I was just on my way to have a look, if you want to come…?"

She is very aware that she's not quite telling the truth – although the stuff about the owl is real. And she is keen to see it again.

"Sure!" Tom says enthusiastically. "I'd love to."

"Great. Follow me."

Neither Mavis nor Tom need telling twice and they walk behind Cecily as she picks her way around the edge of the field, staying close to the hedgerow. They reach an intersection, where there is an opening into the next field, where a bumpy farm track traces an outline around low-level stubble.

"If we head to that tree over there," she says, pointing a little way down the track, "and wait, we might be lucky."

I think I already am, bumping into you. He's always thought Cecily is great, from the moment they met on our first visit to the long barrow. It had just seemed inappropriate to be considering her in a romantic way, at that time. Still, he couldn't help but notice how she was so calm, and natural, and now he finds out she's a bird-lover, too. It was obvious to me, even then. She's just his type, with a nose-ring, and pretty, hazel-coloured eyes. Freckles in the summer, and long, wavy auburn hair, which she mostly keeps tied back.

Again hearing his sisters' voices – like a pair of witches, he thinks fondly – he tries to keep his thoughts chaste, and focused on the owl. Yet under the cover of the bare, gnarled branches, standing as close to Cecily as he can without seeming like some kind of creep, he finds himself all too aware of the sound of her breath, and her scent. What is that, some kind of sandalwood perfume?

Mavis sits between them; just what he needs, another female in his life determined to keep him in check. It will all pay off in the end, Tom.

"There," Cecily breathes, and Tom looks first at her, seeing her soft cheeks pink in the cold of the early morning, then he follows her line of sight and lets out a low whistle as he sees the bird, gliding gracefully over the field. Still moving, it beats its wings a few times then glides again.

"He'll be looking for rodents," Cecily whispers. She looks at Tom. "Sorry, you probably knew that."

He just smiles, not knowing what to say. She is so close that he could lean across and kiss her, but he would never be so presumptuous and besides, their canine chaperone is a barrier between them.

Instead, he returns his gaze to the owl but he is only half focused on it. He's actually considering how pleased he is to have a stirring of desire in himself again. It's been a long time, he thinks: my illness, and my death; his stress, and his grief, have put a dampener on all that.

All too soon, the owl is out of sight, vanishing across the far side of the field.

"I think its nest is over there somewhere," Cecily

says. "I don't want to go too close, but I hope it sticks around. They don't often nest around crops, and this one might just be over-wintering. It would be amazing if they breed here. Have you ever heard one calling? Or wing-clapping? It's so sweet." Cecily is blushing again. She wants to kick herself. "Anyway, I think he might have gone to ground now, and I guess we should probably…" She gestures back towards the long barrow, hoping that Kitty will have gone by now. Cecily is due to be in work at the pub at ten, so she really needs to get going again soon. She had just very much wanted to come to the barrow and light it up for any visitors. This is one of those days she thinks might well be busy.

"Sure," Tom says. "Come on, Mavis." The three of them stride out together and as they round the curve of the field, Cecily sees a figure walking away from them. That almost certainly will be Kitty. She's relieved to find the door locked up and she opens it, then stands back for Tom to go in, vaguely aware of the smell of a recently extinguished candle. She hopes that he won't notice.

"Would you like me to hold Mavis?" she asks. "I can wait outside with her if you like."

"Alright," Tom says. "Thanks."

He uses his phone to light his way, and he takes a lighter from his pocket – he had nearly done this in front of Graham the other day but stopped himself just in time. Even at nearly thirty, he does not want his dad to know he sometimes smokes.

The candle wax is ever-so-slightly soft and warm, but Tom does not notice. His mind is on the girl and the dog waiting for him outside. He feels his own cheeks are warm and his heart is beating fast. He wants to focus on me, but he is finding it difficult.

"Hi Mum," he says, as he lifts the catch on the stained-glass door and opens it. "What do you think?" he whispers conspiratorially.

I think she's perfect for you. I could make the candle flame flicker, as I'd tried to do for Alex on Christmas Day, but I've learned my lesson there. While Alex took it as a sign of my affection for him, what if Tom misreads it, too? Thinks I am warning him off her? I keep my counsel. All I can do is watch, and wait.

He lifts the urn out, cradling it, and carries it outside. Cecily is sitting on one of the carved wooden benches, the spaniel sitting leaning against her leg.

They both turn and look at Tom, Cecily smiling and Mavis wagging her tail.

"Is this stupid?" he asks, half-lifting the urn so she knows what he is referring to.

"No," Cecily says. "Really, no. I think it's lovely."

And she does. She's seen so many people, now, coming to visit – friends and family of we whose ashes reside here. She feels she knows us all individually, as she listens to those who love us tell her stories – sometimes sad, sometimes funny, sometimes incredible. In fact, she knows a lot more about many of us than some of our own family and friends do. She wants to write the stories down, but they are not her tales to tell and she is always extra careful when she's writing to make sure she's not letting somebody else's story seep onto her pages.

Tom sits down, leaving a careful space between the two of them and placing the urn on the other side of him to Cecily. It seems too much to expect her to want it next to her, although of course, being Cecily, she wouldn't mind at all.

"Ruth seemed like a lovely lady," she says now.

"She was. I was very lucky."

"I can't imagine not having my mum around. Well," she corrects herself, "I can try to imagine, but I don't suppose it's possible to know, until it happens."

"No. It's weird," Tom says, caressing Mavis' ears. "It's like – I think we, or I at least, have been preparing for this since I knew it was a possibility. Probability, even. In the natural order of things, our parents will usually die before we do. I saw friends lose a parent and I felt bad for them, but I had no idea what it really meant. It's not just losing somebody who you love so much. It's losing somebody who loves you in a way that nobody else ever will—"

He finds there is a lump in his throat as he voices this thought which he has had so many times, either consciously or subconsciously. He's right. Nobody else is going to love him in the way that I do. But he thinks that love has died with me, and he's wrong about that.

38

"I think I know what you mean." Cecily lays a hand gently on his arm. "I can't say 'I know how you feel', because I don't."

Tom looks at her, grateful for her sensitivity.

"I'm just sorry for you, for all of you. And I'm glad I got to meet your mum."

He sees her eyes are glistening, and finds he wants to hold her, even though it's his grief – his loss – they are feeling.

Instead, he just says, "Thank you." And they sit quietly, contemplatively, companionably, for just a few minutes. Then Cecily stands, goes into the barrow. Busies herself for a while, lighting candles and greeting us all quietly. In time, she hears Tom's footsteps on the gravel, and she sees his silhouette in the barrow doorway.

"I'm just putting Mum back," he says, and finds the words ridiculous. "Then we're going to make a move."

"Alright," Cecily says, and she walks towards him, resting against one of the pillars while he places the urn back in its place, closing and latching the niche cover.

"Thank you," Tom says. "For the owl... and everything."

"My pleasure," Cecily says. "See you again soon." *I hope*, she adds silently.

I hope so, thinks Tom. Then – *Thank you for the owl!* He winces as he recalls his own words. *What an absolute idiot.*

He unties Mavis from the bench and, with her at his side, he turns and walks away, keeping half an eye out for that owl again.

Cecily looks around the barrow and sits once more on the rough-hewn bench. She knows Val will be here soon; probably Derek too – to visit Teresa, no doubt bringing champagne and unseasonal strawberries, alongside their usual good cheer, and she can hand over the care of the barrow to them. For now, she will watch my son and my dog heading back across the fields until they are out of sight. She sits back and thinks over this morning's encounter.

"Thank you for the owl," she says to herself, and she grins.

3

Tom arrives home to find everyone in a strange mood – except for Kitty, who he cannot find at all.

"She's gone," Annie says, matter-of-factly. Unusually it seems that of everyone it is Annie who is in the most upbeat mood.

"Gone," Graham says morosely. "She had to get back to work – that woman's ill." 'That woman' being Meg. Graham has never really taken to her. I think he blames her for Kitty not having a 'real job', which is grossly unfair. All of our children have followed their hearts where work is concerned. It's just that it's only Annie's heart which was set on a challenging, well-paid career, following in Graham's footsteps. I know he worries about their stability, financially, but I think these days everything's so up in the air that stability emotionally is more pressing. Kitty has plenty of that – or she did, until this thing happened with Alex.

Graham would get frustrated with me, if I voiced this opinion to him. I know he thinks, or thought, that I didn't take the material side of things seriously enough. In fact, I always did appreciate just how important it is to have enough money to live on comfortably – even better if you have extra money to be able to enjoy some treats in your life, or follow a passion. But ultimately, how you feel about yourself and your life, and how you treat others, are the things that matter. I know that better than ever now.

"She's not 'that woman'," Tom says, sharing my view on Meg's boss and friend. "She's a great person. What?" He turns to Annie, having heard her 'hrumph'. "She is! You two just don't get her. But she's absolutely dedicated to what she does, and she's sacrificed a lot to look after those animals. She never takes time off, or goes on holiday. And I happen to know she's been a great support to Kitty since Mum got ill."

That's got them. The mention of my name. It's almost funny how in life it slipped off their tongues thoughtlessly: "Mum, have you seen my PE kit?" "Mum, can you give me a lift?" "Mum, can so-and-so come for a sleepover?"

I was at times frustrated by this casual assumption that I was there for their benefit, and their use, although I don't suppose I did much to persuade them otherwise. I worked but I did shifts, and I planned them as much as I could around the children's lives. I tried to make 'my' things have as little impact on family life as possible because above all I wanted to be there for them – but I would perhaps have gone mad without work, or the occasional nights out and trips away with friends.

Now, the mention of my name is met with a little internal jolt; a reminder that I've gone, but I am glad that all of them mention me willingly and frequently. Not for the sake of my ego but because I think it is healthier than to try and avoid the subject. I do also like the thought that they keep me alive that way.

I used to do the same with my own mum and dad, and I remember hoping that someday I would see them again, and my sister, who really died far too young. A friend of mine, a committed shaman, told me very matter-of-factly that I would, and I wanted to believe her, but I was never sure. Now I know. I get it. And if you're wondering, have I seen my parents, and my sister; the friends who came before me? Where are they in all of this? I can tell you, we've been reunited, and it was one of the most joyful experiences I have ever had. An all-encompassing embrace, relief, release, lightness… To describe it fully is difficult, and to explain where they are now even more so.

Why am I in and around the long barrow, and my new friends who also reside there, when I could be with these people who I love so much, and yearned for after they had gone? Well, it's not entirely simple. And I know now that we are together in the most complicated yet most straightforward way, yet we all still have a way to go, and different needs. My priority is my family, and for as long as they need me I will be with them.

At some point, we will be reunited as well, and to

know that is the greatest comfort. But I do not wish them to die, or to cut short their lives on earth. And when I need my parents, my sister, and the other people I have lost throughout my life, I know how to find them. That's about the best way I can explain it right now, and I know it's not quite good enough, but it will have to do.

Graham looks slightly ashamed of himself as he takes in Tom's words. "That's true," he says. "She has been good to Kitty. And she wrote me a lovely letter, after your mum died."

"Who's been good to Kitty?" Alex asks with a nervous feeling in his belly. He comes into the kitchen and stands awkwardly next to Annie, who is sitting on one of the breakfast bar stools. After a moment, he puts his arm around her. She accepts this, Tom notes; she even leans into Alex a bit. That's good to see. He could do without these two annoying each other all day.

"Meg. But she's ill today, apparently," Graham says.

"Why 'apparently'?" Tom is quick to jump back into Meg's corner.

"Oh I don't know," Graham admits, rubbing tired eyes. "I'm not being very fair to her, I realise that. Sorry, Tom. Meg is ill, Alex, and she needed Kitty to go back and cover things at the kennels, I think. I didn't actually see Kitty, she just left this note."

He hands it to Tom, who reads it and puts it on the

counter, seeing nothing untoward in the situation.

Alex tries to peer across at the piece of paper surreptitiously, as if he could read more into Kitty's straightforward words.

Hi Dad,
Sorry to just leave you a note but I didn't want to wake you. I'm afraid Meg's not very well and I'm needed back at the kennels. Give my love to everyone. I will ring you later. Love Kitty xxx
P.S. I know 'happy new year' isn't exactly right at the moment but I do hope this year holds some happy times for you. Love you.

And that's it. Alex is disappointed, somehow, although he can't imagine what she might have said differently. And also he's nursing even more guilt because, once he'd left Kitty's room and met his wife at the top of the stairs, Annie had led him into her bedroom, and begun to kiss him, softly and slowly, looking him in the eye, and he'd found himself unable to resist, once more in thrall to being in his wife's favour. All thoughts – or almost all, at least – of Kitty were banished for a time, as Alex and Annie fell to the bed, in the very room where some years ago they'd first slept together, self-conscious and fumbling and awkward, but giggling with each other, while we – Graham, Kitty, Tom and me – sat downstairs, watching a film. Of course, I didn't know this at the

45

time, and it's one of those things which I think I should not be privy too even now. I'm still learning, how far I should go when it comes to the privacy of the people I love, but that memory is sweet, and Annie thinks of it a lot, which might surprise Alex. She had it in mind as she kissed her husband in the early hours of the brand-new year, as she and he found each other once more.

This is why Annie accepts his arm around her shoulder now. She feels they have connected again, although she also thinks that last night was quite a lot of effort, and she hopes Alex appreciated it.

Alex, who did very much appreciate it, is churning up with guilt and worry; a little bit for Kitty, but mostly at the thought of Annie finding out. That really would mess everything up. It's a stroke of luck, really, that Kitty's boss has fallen ill, and she has had to go.

Don't be dim, Alex, I think.

He is desperate to speak to his sister-in-law but he doesn't want to arouse anyone's suspicions.

"I think I'll make some tea," he says, and he kisses Annie on the forehead before withdrawing his arm and filling the kettle. "And I was thinking I should go and see Mum and Dad in a bit. Wish them a happy new year as well, you know. Do you want to come, Annie?" He knows she won't.

"Yes, of course, I should come and wish them a happy new year as well."

"They'd love that," Alex says, thinking quickly.

46

He'd hoped that a trip to his parents' would provide him with the opportunity to contact Kitty. He makes a pot of tea and pours a cup for each of them.

"Thanks, Alex," Graham says. "I think I'll take mine into the garden. The bird feeders need topping up."

He goes into the utility room, followed by Mavis, and they both walk out into the winter-dull garden, which is brightened by the whistles and calls of the starlings in the huge conifer, and the sight of a robin hopping along the back of a bench.

Ruth? Graham thinks.

No, not quite.

"And I might just go and have a shower," Tom says. "I'm a bit sweaty after the morning's walk."

"I can't believe you've been out already!" Alex says. "New Year's Day is meant to be a chance to recover from the night before."

"I needed to get some air," Tom says. "And I wanted to go and see Mum."

"She's not—" Annie starts to say, but Alex lays a hand on her shoulder.

"I saw an owl," Tom says conversationally.

"Oh yeah?"

"Yes, with, what's her name–?" knowing full well what her name is, and just wanting to mention her – "Cecily."

"My god, does she actually live at the long barrow?" Annie asks, sardonically.

"No, she was just getting the place set up for people

visiting today." Tom's cheeks flush as he leaps to Cecily's defence. Both Annie and Alex see this, and they exchange a quick glance. I am grateful that Annie is in a good enough mood to see her negativity is unwelcome, and unnecessary.

"She does do a great job," she concedes. "And Mum liked her."

"She did, didn't she?" Tom is cheered by this thought, as he takes his cup of tea upstairs.

"Do you think you should maybe stay here with your dad?" Alex asks Annie. "What with Kitty going home? I mean, I know Mum and Dad would be really pleased to see you, but they'll understand if you don't come."

"Don't you want me to come with you?" Annie asks.

"Of course I do!" Alex leaps to a quick self-defence.

"I was just joking," Annie smiles and actually stands to kiss him. She really is surpassing herself. "You might be right, though. Perhaps I'll stay with Dad. Send my love to your folks, though."

"I will." Alex slurps at his tea, which is far too hot. "I might head off soon actually, and then I can be back for lunch."

"Stay with them for lunch if they'd like you to – just do whatever's best."

"Thanks, Annie. I love you."

The fact that Annie is being so nice only adds to his guilt and Alex finds himself wondering if actually she knows what happened, and she's doing all this on purpose to punish him.

Don't be stupid, he tells himself. *Annie's not like that.* He's right. She is far too direct and straight down the line. She always has been. If she knew he had kissed Kitty, she'd have been on his case immediately; Kitty's, too. No, Alex decides, it seems like just bad luck that she's chosen this particular time to decide she likes him again.

Annie, meanwhile, is feeling quite pleased with herself. She remembers the time I spoke to her about the way she treated her husband. "Alex clearly loves you, and for good reason. We all love you, for that matter. You are unique, and intelligent, and fierce and strong. But you need to understand that not everyone is the same, and also that you don't have to be always fierce and strong, and especially not around us. And perhaps a little less so towards Alex."

She has made a new year's resolution, although she is not telling anyone what it is. She thinks she is going to try and live a bit more like I did, try to be a little more like me. The thought of this touches me so deeply and makes me yearn to be able to hold her and talk to her, properly, so she can hear me.

"I wasn't perfect," I want to say, but I know she doesn't think I was. And I have to admit, it's gratifying to know that my words as a mother were listened to occasionally. The resolution begins with her being nicer to Alex and trying to give him less of a hard time. Granted, we are only a few hours into the new year but so far, so good.

Nevertheless, when Alex leaves the house, Annie is pleased to have some space, and glad that he suggested she didn't need to visit her in-laws. She goes into the lounge and lies on the settee, switching on the TV to some classic New Year's Day TV. In time, Graham comes and joins her and, unusually, Mavis selects her to cuddle into. Annie is quietly pleased about this, and glad of the spaniel's warmth against her. As Graham gets a fire going, then resumes his seat from the night before, tending to the flames and the logs, he glances across to see his daughter has fallen asleep – the dog too – and he feels an overwhelming tenderness sweep through him.

4

"You've reached Kitty's phone. Sorry I can't take your call. Leave me a message and I'll get back to you as soon as I can."

Alex thumps the dashboard. Why had he assumed she'd be available, or even that she would want to talk to him? He's pulled up around the corner from his parents' house and has a few minutes to spare before they're expecting him. Will Kitty call back? He sits and waits. Nothing.

But she'll be busy, won't she? Looking after the dogs. Or maybe looking after that boss of hers, if she's not very well.

"Dammit," says Alex. He checks the time. He needs to get to his parents'. Kitty is going to have wait.

Anyway, just because she hasn't answered, it doesn't necessarily mean she's avoiding him.

Except, she is.

Kitty sees Alex's name on her phone screen. She knew, or she thought she did, that he would ring, but she has absolutely no idea what to say to him, so she chooses not to pick up. She needs to talk this through with someone; needs some good, solid advice before she does or says anything she might regret.

Anything else *I might regret*, she corrects herself.

She has just arrived at the kennels and is keen to see Meg. Switching her phone to silent, she opens the car door, happy as always to be back in this special place.

While Alex sits in the car, composing one WhatsApp message after another, but sending none of them, Meg opens the door to her office and ushers Kitty inside. "What's up then, my good friend?" she asks, and Kitty falls into her open arms, and begins to cry.

In the stuffy room, Meg waits for Kitty to calm down, and then she makes her sit in the big desk chair while she puts on the kettle in Tea Corner, as she and Kitty call the tiny space allocated to mugs and a box of tea bags. "Go on then," she says. "Tell Aunty Meg what this is all about."

"Oh god," Kitty says, her head in her hands. "Oh god, oh god, oh god." She feels she is being dramatic. It reminds her, in fact, of her behaviour straight after I had died, when she'd sat with my body, and everything she had done – every noise she emitted, every action she made – felt like it was for somebody else's benefit. Like she had an unseen audience. Now, she has a genuine audience, and she feels suddenly childish and stupid.

She pulls herself up straight. Looks Meg in the eye. "I kissed Alex."

"Alex…" Meg looks puzzled for a moment and Kitty can see the moment when the name registers properly. Her eyes widen. "*Alex?*"

"Yes. I know, I know. Fucking hell."

"But how…? Why…?" Meg knows of Alex from Kitty's stories of him, and although Kitty is fond of her brother-in-law, she is not always very kind in her depiction of him.

"I don't know!" Kitty nearly wails, but stops herself. *Don't make any more of this than you have to*, she cautions herself. "He's… he's been very kind to me, over Christmas. And you remember at Mum's funeral… I suppose I've seen another side to him lately."

"You're vulnerable, Kitty!" Meg says angrily. "He's taking advantage."

"Oh no, I don't think… I don't think it's like that. He's not like that."

"They're all like that," Meg says grimly.

"Well, I don't know if I agree with you there," Kitty thinks of Tom, and her dad, who are the best men she knows, "but anyway, no, honestly, I don't think Alex is taking advantage. It wasn't planned, I don't think. We just… Annie was being her usual self with him, and I'd gone upstairs with Mavis – the fireworks, you know–" Meg nods sagely – "and then Alex came up, just to wish me happy new year – don't look like that! – and the next thing I know, we're kissing."

"Did he kiss you, or did you kiss him?"

"I think he kissed me. I mean, it really lasted no

more than two seconds, if that. I could almost persuade myself it didn't happen. Except it did."

"Hmm."

"Hmm?"

"Just thinking. Did you talk about it afterwards?"

"No. Annie came upstairs. And I chickened out this morning, just left a note and ran. Actually, I went to the long barrow first, then came straight here. He has... he's just tried to call me, actually."

"You didn't answer?" Meg puts two cups of steaming lemon and ginger tea on the desk, creating wet circles on the papers that are strewn across it.

"No, I... what do I say?"

"You say," Meg speaks decisively, "that it was a huge mistake and you both need to pretend it never happened."

"Do you think we can?"

"Yes. More than that, you have to. He's your brother-in-law, for Christ's sake."

"I know that!"

"So go back to what you said before – you could almost convince yourself it never happened. Convince yourself."

"What if he wants to take it further?"

"Well, do you?"

"No! Absolutely not."

"Then it never happened."

Kitty nods. This is good advice, she thinks. Perhaps the only advice, if she doesn't want her world to fall apart any more than it already has. She's lost me, she's lost Olly. She cannot lose Annie – and potentially Graham and Tom as well. What on earth would they make of what's happened?

Why are humans so stupid? she wonders. She and Alex both. They had acted on some urge – she's not sure exactly what, even, because she's fairly certain she's not really attracted to him – without a thought for the wider implications. Her sister, her dad, her brother… Alex's parents… there are ripples, she sees clearly now, which radiate from this kind of action, and what has started with a simple, brief kiss has the potential to make those ripples grow into something bigger, becoming waves which could upset so many people, send them completely off-balance.

Meg is right, she decides firmly. The best thing to do is nothing. Forget the whole thing and pretend it never happened. First, though, she's going to have to speak to Alex.

"Kitty?" he whispers, aware that he is in earshot of his mum and dad. "I can't talk now, can I call you back?"

"OK," she says.

"I'll be literally about five minutes," he says. "That OK?"

"Sure."

She is aware that it's unfair of her to have expected him to be ready to talk when she was. Thinking he is probably still at our place, she imagines that Annie will be around somewhere, maybe Tom and Graham as well. Still, she'd got herself primed for this conversation and the delay wasn't something she'd planned on.

She sits in the office, while Meg busies herself letting some of the dogs out into their runs, and drums her fingers on the desk.

It's not a bad place, the kennels, and I wish I'd come to visit when I was alive. I suppose you don't tend to visit your children's places of work, as a rule, but Kitty did ask Graham and me once, she was clearly so enthused by it – particularly the rescue side of things – and I did mean to, but... well, no excuses. I just didn't get round to it. I suppose it always made sense to me that the children would come back to us rather than us going to them, and there's no space in Kitty's flat for us to stay over. Plus, if I'm honest, I didn't really relish the prospect of us visiting when Olly was around. We did go to their flat, of course – more than once – but usually we would tie those visits in with something else, so as not to outstay our welcome. I never felt particularly welcomed by Olly, and at least when they came to see us at home there was a bit more space for us all, to keep frustrations at bay, and prevent tempers from fraying.

The office is warm, and tidy aside from the piles of papers on the desk. It is not a big space, but Meg keeps it very clean – I suppose she really needs to if she sleeps in here as well – and there's a very relaxed, comforting feel to the space. Kitty tries to breathe it all in, and remain composed and in control as she awaits the return phone call. Thankfully, Alex doesn't keep her waiting.

"Kitty!" he says as she answers, his own relief evident.

"Hi," she replies flatly, finding her heart is beating fast against her chest.

"Are you alright?"

"Yes, are you?"

"I… yes, thank you."

This is not how it's meant to go. Kitty has planned her speech, she does not want long-winded, polite small talk.

"We need to talk," she says. "Well, I need to."

"Of course, of course." Alex nervously awaits what his sister-in-law is about to say. Is she secretly in love with him? Has she been, all along?

"It was a terrible mistake," Kitty blurts out and then, more carefully, "I mean, I really care about you, Alex, but you must know as well as I do that we shouldn't have done that. It shouldn't have happened." She is being generous, knowing that she could have said 'you shouldn't have done that', but she does not wish to sound accusing. She just wants this whole mess to go away.

"I feel exactly the same," he says, and they both experience an intense relief. He's very fond of her, but now he's back in Annie's good books, and now this…

thing... has happened, he knows that his feelings for Kitty are not what he imagined. And besides, he is scared of Annie, of incurring her wrath. I don't blame him.

"So... everything's really OK?" Kitty laughs.

"Yes, I... I think so," he says tentatively.

"I mean, I know we shouldn't have... that shouldn't have... but it was a weird night. It's been a weird few months."

"I couldn't agree more," he says, eager to find common ground and move this situation on now. "And I know we shouldn't have – but we didn't really, I mean, it was barely —"

"Alex," Kitty says firmly.

"Yes?"

"I think it's best if we just don't talk about it. Never mention it again. Forget it's happened."

"Sure, sure," Alex agrees. "That's a very sensible idea."

"OK. Well, thanks," she says, though she doesn't know what she's thanking him for.

"No problem," he accepts her gratitude unquestioningly.

"Bye then," Kitty says, finding herself exhausted and with nothing left to say.

"Bye, Kitty. See you soon."

And they both hang up. Alex returns to his parents' living room and his mum is aware that he seems much happier and less on edge than when he'd arrived.

"Was that Annie?" Celia asks, knowing that he and Annie have a slightly fraught relationship. She had been slightly put out, though not surprised, that her daughter-in-law had not come to visit today.

"What? Er... yeah."

"Everything OK?"

"It is now," he says, without thinking.

"Oh?"

"Oh, er, nothing. Just a strange time, what with Ruth..."

"Of course, of course."

Alex stays a few minutes more then takes his leave, promising to pop in and see his mum and dad during the week.

When he's gone, his mum turns to his dad: "Did Alex seem alright, do you think?"

"He was fine. Wasn't he?" James, like Alex, is not always quite on the ball when it comes to picking up on other people's feelings and moods.

"He was after that phone call," she says. "I wonder who it was. I do worry about him, you know. I hope he's happy."

"He's fine," James says. "I'm sure he is."

"I hope so."

And, for the time being, he is. Alex drives back to our place to pick up Annie.

"I'll see you next weekend, Dad," Annie promises before they leave, kissing Graham on the cheek. She even hugs Tom – a rare occurrence.

My husband and son wave Alex and Annie off from the driveway.

"And then there were two," Graham says. It's the kind of thing Tom finds very hard to bear. Nevertheless, being a kind son, he puts his arm around his dad and walks him back into the house.

It seems strange, now that the others have gone, and the decorations seem out of place and pointless.

"Shall we take this lot down?" Tom suggests.

"Yes, why not?" agrees Graham. Something else to keep him busy. Keep him going till teatime. Then he can get to work in the kitchen, cooking, then eating, then clearing up, then a bit of TV, then bed. If he plots out his days like this – divides them into easy-to-manage segments – he finds he can just about get by.

Tom puts some music on and the two of them set to work, taking more time than necessary in unfurling the lights from the banisters then working as a team to wind them up carefully so that they don't get tangled. Tom takes the pile of Christmas cards into the lounge, meaning to read them this evening. There will be messages in them; carefully chosen words for this first Christmas after my death, and he feels the need to appreciate them – and reply on behalf of the family, where appropriate. He knows Graham is not up to the job. I'm proud of him.

The tinsel comes down, and the tree; baubles are packaged gently. Neither Tom nor Graham do much talking but they're companionable enough. When the last decoration is packed away, they carry everything upstairs and Tom pulls down the loft ladder, climbing up and waiting for Graham to pass him the boxes so that he can put them away until next time.

"All done," he says, when the last one is in, and he feels a relief at closing the loft hatch, shutting away the gaping blackness of the roof space.

Graham, it seems, feels the same, and has switched on the landing lights, closing the curtains against the incoming winter night.

"Tea?" Graham asks.

"Why not?" Tom replies agreeably. "I'll go and check on the fire." Into the warmth of the lounge he goes, drawing the thick curtains and noting that the fire needs some prodding to really get going again. The poker provokes a few sparks, and soon there are flames again. Tom is reminded of the candles at the long barrow, which leads his thoughts to Cecily, who is not far from his mind anyway, and he smiles.

Graham, in the kitchen, leans against one of the counters, breathing slowly, as he's trying to remember to do when it all gets too much.

That's it then, he thinks. *Christmas done and dusted.* It had not been as bad as he'd dreaded but, he considers, this is just the beginning. As he pulls the kitchen blinds closed, he casts one last look outside, seeing nothing but darkness.

5

I used to dread January. When I was at school, and had to get up in the dark, and return in the dark, and nobody had any money – and the joy and good will of Christmas was all but gone – Judy and I would hole ourselves up in our room, with the small number of toys we had received for Christmas, and we'd create make-believe worlds, using our bedcovers as snow-covered plains or vast desert landscapes.

As we grew older, and we moved into a new, bigger house, where we each had a bedroom, I would come home and snuggle under the covers with a book for company, trying my best to appreciate the good side of winter, as my mum, and the vicar, and Sunday School teacher, said that we should.

"Each day on God's good earth is a blessing," I would remind myself piously, but it was hard to feel it sometimes, when even the inside of the windows was laced with frost and ice.

We were not well off, growing up, and throughout my life it has helped to remind myself of this. Including during those winters once I was married, and a mother, and I had central heating, and a lovely bright kitchen; a TV in the lounge, and a phone upstairs and downstairs. I would mourn the death of each Christmas and New Year period, which I loved so much, and had looked forward to for so long, but I would pull myself together.

I no longer believed in that concept of God, and how we must be grateful for literally everything we experience – good and bad – but I had managed to hold onto the idea that it is good to appreciate what we have, and I could not help but acknowledge that what I had was much more than many others. I had to count myself lucky. And I also had to try and show the children how lucky they were. With a warm, secure family home, and parents who loved them; never any doubt as to where their next meal would be coming from, and support for their education and other interests.

It meant that when they became morose at the idea of returning to school, or just the loss of those cosy, lazy Christmas holiday days, I would gently berate them and remind them to enjoy every day as best as they could – all while inwardly struggling to keep to this myself. I knew full well how they felt, and I shared the struggle of those cold dark mornings, prising our eyes open and unbundling ourselves from sleep-warmed duvets. I sympathised. But it was my job to keep them going.

Now, I see things slightly differently. Out at the long barrow while the sharp wind cuts straight across the fields, sending songbirds into hiding amid the bare branches and twigs of the trees and hedgerows, I feel the necessity of winter. It has a hard job to undertake. It accepts its unpopular reputation and that it will never be loved, at least not by many, as much as spring with all its promise, and summer with those long, hazy, light-filled days; even autumn, with its heart-warming, breath-taking colours.

No, winter has to work harder than any other season, and it forms the basis for all those other joyful days. Like so many hard workers, it is under-appreciated but even so, it has the capacity to throw forth a handful of stand-out, gleaming days, and this is one such day.

It means that the long barrow is busy, or the busiest it has been since New Year. I'm lucky to have two visitors myself, though glad that they don't coincide. This is thanks to Nick. He had planned to come and visit before lunch but, having pulled into the car park and recognised my car, he reconsiders his plans, and pulls back onto the road. He will travel on to the supermarket, do his weekly shop and perhaps have some lunch; hopefully the sunshine and clear skies will hold for the afternoon.

Graham has taken to driving my car more than his own. To him, it still smells of me, and it's another one of those physical connections to the person that I was.

He gets out of it now, dusting some mud off the doorframe and muttering to himself. It makes me smile; he'll focus on something like this rather than face up to the actual reason he's feeling put out. I say 'put out'; I don't suppose that really begins to cover how he feels. He's heartbroken. Bereft. Lost at sea. He too struggles with the cold, dark loneliness of January, and he has taken to sleeping in later and later. Really, he thinks, what is the point of getting out of bed? It just means more hours to fill.

This morning, though, at the sight of the bright light leaking through the gap in the curtains, he's given himself a mental kick, and got himself out of bed; showered – quietly, because Tom was on a late shift last night – and made himself a boiled egg for breakfast. As is often the case, when it came to actually eating anything he's cooked, Graham found his mouth dry and his appetite shrivelled up, but he forced himself to eat most of the egg, and the two pieces of toast, then took himself off to brush his teeth and check over his outward appearance. It's something he likes to do before he comes to the long barrow, almost like he's coming on a date. I find it both sweet and heartrending. Now more than ever I realise outward appearances mean nothing, but I do understand how it can make you feel better; more self-assured, and more outwardly confident, if you feel like you look your best.

He smoothed a wayward eyebrow with his fingertip,

pulled gently at the saggy skin underneath his eyes, and sighed. Slapping on a bit of aftershave, he thought, *It will have to do.*

Now, he is vaguely aware of the car that pulls onto the car park then out again, but he's opening the boot, pulling out his wellies, and my old walking rucksack complete with woolly hat and gloves. He puts the hat on, memories flicking through his mind of the numerous times I'd done the same. Does it matter that he is putting on a woman's hat, he wonders. Will anyone notice? Would anyone care? He pulls on the gloves too, which are a snug fit, then slides his feet out of his driving shoes and into his wellies. To try and ram them into my boots would be a step too far (no pun intended).

Closing and locking the car, Graham emits a "Brrr," for his own benefit it would seem, and makes a brisk start on the walk across the road and along the hard, brown path. To his right, a huge gang of jackdaws bicker and chatter, rising up from the land and making for the trees at the far end of the field. Smaller brown birds flit amongst the shorn remnants of last year's yields. Are they thrushes? Field fares? Tom would know. Graham wishes he had brought his binoculars.

He sees two figures walking towards him and thinks he recognises them from Christmas. That woman and, presumably, her son, who organised the carols. His shoulders hunch involuntarily. He doesn't feel like talking to anyone. The mammoth effort involved in conversation, particularly with people he doesn't really know, seems to wipe him out these days. As he and they approach each other, he sees they are smiling but, confident and gregarious as they are, they seem also to be sensitive and thoughtful and perhaps realise this is not a time to chat.

Val and Derek merely wish Graham a good morning and, relieved, he returns the greeting then continues on his way. He picks up his pace again, and looks around him once more, seeing the standing water in the next field; admiring the golden hue of the dried long grasses in the place where multitudes of wildflowers grow during spring and summer. A wind turbine quietly goes about its business; its white body and blades sharp against the blunt colours of winter.

At the barrow, Graham stops and breathes. *Be still my beating heart*, he thinks, though the context is not appropriate. He pushes the numbers on the lock and he leaves the vivid daylight behind him, entering the softness of the chambers. *It's like being unborn*, he thinks, then tells himself to stop being so melodramatic. Fumbling for the box of matches, his hand finds them, and he picks up one of the spare tea lights, striking a match and lighting the small candle's wick so that he can find his way to 'me'.

It is not difficult, and the sunshine eases subtly into the chamber anyway, but there is something comforting in holding a light, no matter how small.

Hello Ruth, he thinks. Graham can rarely bring himself to speak aloud here. He thinks that if I can hear him, I can hear his thoughts just as well as I could hear any spoken words. He's right.

Hello Graham, I respond, but I don't think he is aware.

He examines the stained-glass door and its image of our family, but makes no effort to open it or take out the urn. Interestingly, of all my family, Graham is the one who least believes that it is me in there. Maybe because he's older – wiser, or closer to his own death – or perhaps because he saw first-hand my physical self failing while mentally, emotionally, spiritually I remained the same person. All three of our children were with us as much as they could be, and Tom was living with us so I suppose he also saw the gradual process more clearly than the girls did but we tried to shield him as much as we could.

Still, this place of focus is important to my husband. He sits now, heavily, on the stone seat below the niches, and he hunches over. He's not crying. He wouldn't say he is past that, but it's more like he doesn't even have that kind of energy anymore. It's like everything has been drained from him. Just putting one foot in front of the other is the most enormous effort, if he thinks too much about it.

And now he's praying – in a way. He, like me, is not religious, but was brought up that way, and so we have both found ourselves falling back on prayer, when every other option seems worn out. Now, he does not know what to pray for. Just that I am OK. That the kids are OK. He doesn't really care whether he is OK. It's just not important. For his own sake, he'd die now, but he has a very fundamental understanding that for our family this would be so much the wrong thing.

Just keep them safe, he thinks. *Please.*

And he closes his eyes; safe, alone, in the barrow. He closes his eyes, and his head drops to his chest, and he pushes himself to remember me: my face; my voice; my smile. He thinks back to when we first met; our first date; bringing me home to meet his mother; our wedding… our honeymoon… The sweetness of those memories is real, and I find myself looking back with him, wishing that he knew.

We were besotted with each other and told ourselves again and again how lucky we were. We had put a deposit on a house, and we moved in on our return from honeymoon, finding that our sisters had been there before us, putting flowers in vases and dinners in the fridge – alongside a bottle of champagne from Graham's boss. We came back home to a house full of love, and I thought I could never be unhappy again.

I wouldn't change a thing, I want to say to him. I want him to know. Not even the thing with his secretary. I really was as lucky to find my husband as I thought back then at the beginning.

As the memories and images creep through his mind, Graham actually nods off. He falls asleep! Sitting here in the barrow. My friends in death creep across towards us. Kiran smiles at him, as you might a sleeping baby. "He's so peaceful," she says.

"He is," I agree. "He needs this."

And, strange though it may sound, we surround him; Kiran, Teresa, Terry, June, Adam and Jasmine. We've become quite a little family here in the barrow. While Graham sleeps, we sit with him, watching him. Breathing with him. Trying to reach him somehow, to soothe him. After twenty minutes or so, when he wakes with a jolt, once he's remembered where he is and realised that he's dozed off, he feels somehow better than he did before. Still utterly lonely and heartbroken, but refreshed in a way he hasn't felt for some time.

He blinks his eyes in the darkness, the small tealight still burning loyally at his side. He listens, to the silence of the long barrow. For a moment he wonders what he would do if he heard a noise, from further in, from the depths of the second chamber. But there is nothing. Not even the dripping of water that one might expect in this place which is reminiscent of a cave.

Standing, he stretches. Looks towards the door; picks up on the birdsong. The cawing of those jackdaws. There is life out there. He finds he wants to see it. He looks towards the niche, then back towards the outside world. *Back soon, Ruth*, he thinks, then he steps forwards, out of the darkness and into the light. Setting the lock on the door, he strides straight ahead, along the causeway towards the amphitheatre. He is not ready for home yet. He wants to go a little further.

When Graham returns, he sees a man sitting on the bench outside the barrow. Nick. In life, my heart would have been in my throat at this encounter, but now I have to trust to fate, to see what it will bring.

"Hi," Graham says. He recognises this man. They passed each other on Christmas Day.

"Hello," says Nick, showing no sign of recognition. "Lovely day."

"That it is," Graham says, and leaves him to it.

Did he think it odd that Nick hadn't gone into the barrow? I know Nick is wondering about this but Graham seems determined to keep his own sense of positivity flowing, he does not want to give another thought to the stranger sitting on the bench. He walks on, and heads back to the car, and Nick relaxes.

He'd seen that my car was still parked up, of course, but decided he couldn't leave and come back yet again. He'd just have to walk up to the barrow and back if Graham was inside. When he got here to find the door locked but no sign of Graham, he worried for a moment, for my husband's wellbeing. It is not at all uncommon for bereavement to bring on thoughts of suicide. But he used his doctor's sense of realism, and calm. Decided to sit for a while. *The man has probably just gone for a walk*, he thought, and of course he was right. Now, with Graham gone and the barrow still locked, Nick does not have the code and he cannot get in but he, like Graham, is also of the opinion that what is within the barrow, stored in the urn within the niche, is not me. He does not even really believe that I am anything more than the memories which hold me. But he likes this place, and he appreciates the focal point, of somewhere to come and to think and remember – again just as Graham does. The two of them have far more in common than I'd ever thought.

He's not afraid to speak to me, though – never thinking I can actually hear him, but finding solace in saying words aloud. Who else can he confide in?

"Ruth," he says now, and louder again: "Ruth. How I miss you."

I know, I think. *I know you do*. And I wish, not for the first time, that I had never allowed whatever it was that we had to continue. But, selfishly, I had needed him. I had wanted him.

"It's all a bit quiet now," he says. "I can't be bothered with any of it. I met up with Isabel last week –" Isabel was a girlfriend of Nick's, who he'd seen for a while a couple of years back; we weren't officially having an affair, and even if we had been, I was still married, so would have had no leg to stand on when it came to him seeing other people – "but it all just felt so flat. She doesn't know, of course, that I'm grieving. I think

I just depressed her. Anyway, I haven't heard from her since." He laughs. "And I couldn't care less. The thing is, she's not you."

Nick looks out now, along the straight line of the causeway, where Graham had walked not so long ago. His eyes narrow as he searches the horizon, though he doesn't know what he's looking for.

"Anyway," he continues, "I can't just stop everything. I can't. And if I don't want a girlfriend then I do want to work. I miss it, in a different way to missing you. And maybe, it sounds stupid, but maybe I think I'll find something of you there. I'm going back. I'm not over the hill yet. Not quite."

This is not news to me, but I'm glad he's come to tell me. It was one of our shared passions, work, and we were a good team if we happened to be treating the same patient. It was how we connected in the first place.

Good for you, I tell him. *Good for you*. And he does look around, like he's heard something, but he's just trying to make sure nobody's approaching, to hear him talking to himself.

He gets up and walks across to the barrow, steps inside the doorway, though he can go no further. He can see into the curve of the first chamber, where the soft daylight leaking in makes the covering of my niche just visible. He does not resent that happy family scene depicted there but he does wonder if he and I could have created something just as good, if life had worked out differently.

I have no idea, and I try not to think that way. Life happened as it did, and I have three beautiful children, thanks to Graham; and I've left behind a close family unit (well, until Alex stuck his oar in), so I don't want to think about the alternative lives I might have lived.

Teresa is at my side. She wraps me in her warmth. "It's not easy," she says.

Nick leans in, and listens; like Graham, he's intrigued to discover what secrets the barrow might hold, but all is quiet within. He looks all the way through to the full-length stained-glass door at the other end of the barrow. It is glowing in the afternoon light, meaning that the day is getting on. Although the earth is on the turn towards longer days, it will be a while before we really feel their effect.

"I'd better go," he says, though he doesn't know why, or where. "Shopping to get back," he explains, thinking practically. "See you soon," he addresses the space before him vaguely then steps back into the afternoon.

Hands in pockets, he walks purposefully back along the path, passing nobody on his way. He admires the sunlight on the standing water, and stops for a moment to watch the way that the starlings group and regroup in the vast stretch of sky before descending and settling in the trees which the jackdaws had earlier occupied. Then he walks on, my handsome, lonely doctor, back to the road and across to the car park, climbing into his pristine, empty vehicle and driving back to his equally empty home.

6

Annie exhales slowly, her back to Alex. They are in the kitchen and she's preparing a curry, using the recipe book he bought her for Christmas. It is already dark outside, and Annie had a vision in her head of a couple of hours cooking, in her own company. She likes the methodical chopping of vegetables; the sizzling and scent of them in the pan; she even enjoys clearing away the mess and washing up, putting the kitchen back to its usual spick and span state. Creating order from mess. Often, she will be listening to an audiobook (non-fiction), or Radio 4. It's as close as she comes to mindfulness, I suppose, until Alex decides to get involved.

"It'll be nice to cook together," he says, washing his hands and rolling up his sleeves, seeing nothing wrong – in fact, everything right – with wanting to spend time with his wife. As ever, he is not seeing *her*; not looking at what she wants. His is a very black-and-white view of the world: if you're married to each other, you should want to be together. End of. His own parents do everything together, so I suppose he models his idea of relationships on theirs. Besides, despite his and Kitty's agreement to pretend the kiss never happened, he is still feeling guilty. And he's scared that Annie knows somehow, or that she'll find out. Staying close to her means he can feel reassured that everything is OK.

"What am I doing with these onions again?" he asks.

"Like I said," she tries not to sound too exasperated, whilst thinking *like I said three times already*, "they need to be chopped fine. Look, you can read the recipe if you want to."

"No, no, you're much better at all this than me. Just tell me what you need me to do."

I need you to go and sit in the lounge and watch TV, she thinks. But she smiles. "Just chop those up nice and fine, and put the peel in the green bin. Then you can go and chill, if you like. Or sort out that washing you said you needed to do."

"No, no, I don't expect you to do all the cooking." Alex is sure he is being the perfect, thoughtful husband. "I can't just go and sit on my arse while you're in here slaving away."

"Well why don't you sort the washing, then?" Annie says as sweetly as she can, channelling Kitty. "Honestly, I've got this covered. You know I like cooking, anyway."

"Trying to get rid of me, are you?"

Annie, though she is not the most emotionally literate, does know that Alex is only half-joking when he says this. She sees the doubt on his face, and feels sorry for him.

"Of course I'm not! Look, you get on with the onions, and I'll do the squash, then maybe you can get the spices we need."

"Great." The boyish smile on his face gets her. She is trying very hard to be more thoughtful, and understanding. And OK, she tells herself, maybe she'd been looking forward to a couple of hours in the kitchen, but isn't it better that he doesn't just expect her to do everything?

"I was going to listen to an audiobook though, do you mind if I put it on?"

"Why don't we listen to some tunes instead?" Alex suggests, fiddling with his phone. "Here, I'll put something on."

He is trying his best, but he's missing the point again, and again. Still, Annie tells herself, it's not all about her. She smiles and returns to the task in hand, peeling the squash.

I have to say, I'm impressed with my daughter. Understanding and sensitivity are not very high up her main list of qualities, so she really is putting the effort in. And Alex is trying his very best to do the right thing. If I didn't know what had happened between him and Kitty, I'd think perhaps things between these two could be on the up.

"Dad rang earlier," Annie says while she and Alex eat the curry. He's set the table and lit a candle, and changed the music to something classical. It's sweet, really, she thinks, trying to overlook his enthusiastic chewing and the fact he's managed to help himself to way more than half of the naan bread, leaving her with the burnt bit (the naan had been his responsibility, but he'd been busy trying to find 'the nice wine' and had forgotten to get it out of the oven on time).

"Oh yeah?" he says, not overly interested.

"He said he's worried about Kitty."

At this, Alex looks up. Is she leading somewhere? Has this whole thing – the cooking together, the romantic table setting (overlooking the fact that both of these things were in fact his doing) – just been a way of lulling him into a false sense of security? What does Graham know?

"Why?" Alex asks, in as nonchalant a way as he can.

"He says he's hardly heard from her – and she's not coming back to visit like she was doing."

"Well, maybe she's trying to get back to normal a bit," Alex suggests, relieved. "She didn't used to come back all that much, did she? Before Ruth was ill, I mean."

"No, I suppose not."

"Perhaps it's her new year's resolution or something." He laughs nervously at the link with New Year but Annie doesn't notice.

"It could be, I guess. Anyway, I spoke to Tom, and

we've decided we'll go across and see her next weekend. Just to make sure that's she's alright."

"Oh, right."

"Is that OK? We haven't got any plans, have we?"

"Of course it's OK!" Alex laughs again. "She's your sister, isn't she? Do you want me to come?"

"No, no, that's fine. Tom says he'll drive, and it might be fun, to have a bit of sibling time, you know."

"That sounds nice," Alex says, his brain whirring away. He recalls Kitty's words: "I think it's best if we just don't talk about it. Never mention it again. Forget it's happened."

There is no way, he reasons, that she's going to want to rock the boat. Still, he finds he is suddenly not all that hungry, and although he manages to finish his curry, he leaves most of his naan bread untouched. Annie has left hers too, he sees. What a waste.

He clears the table, leaving everything on the worktop. He is on edge, and finds the guilt he'd thought he had banished had actually just been hiding away for a while. It's making itself known again and Alex is aware of an uncomfortable feeling in his stomach. "I'd better go and sort that washing," he says.

Off he goes, leaving Annie to clear up, but she doesn't really mind. She finally has the kitchen to herself and she can put everything back in place, and listen to her audiobook in peace.

7

Kitty sees his car before he spots her. Her stomach drops. *Oh no.* Alex has parked on the street outside her flat. She can see his dark hair sticking up above the top of his headrest. Her heart beats faster.

A sunburst of possibilities explodes in her mind. What if he's come to tell her that Annie knows about the kiss? What if he's come to declare his undying love for her? She's been lonely, she realises, and for the briefest of moments this idea seems like it could even be appealing, but as soon as it's in her mind it's gone again.

Then, more worrying than anything, she wonders what if it's nothing to do with what happened between them, and something's happened to Annie, or their dad, or Tom? She's not been great at keeping in touch with them these last few weeks: a combination of guilt, and just needing time to herself, to let things settle. It's been hard to garner the energy required to have a 'normal' conversation, and so she has largely avoided it – hoping that the odd WhatsApp message will be enough to cover communication between her and her family. If something has happened to them – and now that she's seen what happened to me, she knows that it can, it could… there is no more 'things happen to other people' for Kitty – she will never forgive herself for being so pathetic.

Shoulders back, she marches across to the car, and knocks on the window more vociferously than she had intended to. It makes Alex jump and he looks at her, shocked. An expression of fear briefly crosses his features and then something like relief. Despite everything, he is pleased to see her. He starts to wind down his window, then thinks better of it and opens his door, gets out of the car.

"Hi," he says, offering Kitty a chaste peck on the cheek.

"Is everything OK?" she asks, without a greeting.

"Erm, I don't know."

Her heartbeat picks up pace again. "What do you mean you don't know? What is it? Is it Dad?"

Understanding registers on Alex's face. "No. Oh, no, Kitty, sorry, it's nothing like that."

A flood of relief. Kitty feels like her shoulders have collapsed. Her legs feel shaky. She must always be on edge at the moment, she realises. Always expecting the worst. I wish I could prop her up. Support her. As ever, I can only watch.

"What is it, then?" she asks, her directness reminding me of her older sister. Kitty is not the pushover that people sometimes assume.

"It's… can we go in…?" Alex gestures towards Kitty's flat, adding sheepishly, "I'm dying for the loo."

"Of course," she says. "But what is it? Why have you come here, with no warning?"

"Sorry," Alex says, walking quickly with ever-increasing pressure on his bladder now he knows relief is near. "I should have called, but you never answer."

"I was at work," she says, sidestepping the correct accusation that she wouldn't have answered his call anyway. "You could have messaged."

"Yes, well I suppose I was halfway here before I'd decided I should definitely come."

"So…?" Kitty looks at him while she pushes her front door key into her lock.

"Can I just go for a wee?" he asks. "Then we can talk."

Kitty does not like the sound of this. Has he left Annie? Does he want her instead? That would be impossible. And not what she would want anyway. "Go on then," she says begrudgingly, and she leaves him to it, pulling off her boots and padding through to the small open-plan kitchen and living area, where she puts her kettle on and pulls her shoulders back once more.

The sound of the toilet flush and Alex fumbling with the lock, then he is with her.

"Tea?" she asks.

"Yes please."

"Sugar?"

"Kitty, even I'm not stupid enough to think you don't remember how I have my tea."

"Sorry."

"That's OK. And it's me who should be sorry. You're absolutely right, I shouldn't have just turned up like this. Only, I wanted to warn you, that you're going to receive another visit, at the weekend."

"Oh?"

"Yes, you're going to be ambushed, by Annie and Tom."

"OK…"

"They're worried about you. Your dad is, too. And so am I. But at least I know why you're keeping your distance… or I think I do."

"Yes, well it's been a bit weird, hasn't it, since New Year?" She hands him a cup of tea.

"Yes, but I thought we'd sorted that. Agreed it never happened…?"

He doesn't want her, then. Is she disappointed? Only her ego, slightly dented. This is the best thing, she knows that.

"Yes, but that's easier said than done. And no, Alex-" she sees him about to say something; knows what he's thinking – "I'm not in love with you, or anything of the sort. It's just that saying it never happened is easier than actually believing it. Besides, it's been good to have some space. To think about Mum, and how I feel about it all, without having to consider anyone else's feelings."

"I can see that. It's hard, isn't it? You're all so close. You all care about each other so much."

"Yes." Kitty is surprised by the tears which spring up. "We do. But I don't think I've processed it all yet, or even really begun to. It helps me, being here, getting stuck into work at the kennels, and I've been really pushing my painting lately, too."

"Have you? Can I see?"

"Sure." Kitty is pleased to have somebody showing an interest. She knows her family think she is a good painter but they don't really believe she can make it, or make a living from it. I was guilty of that myself, and I wish I'd been more supportive. She has to find her own belief within and she tells herself regularly that if it can happen for other people, there's no reason it shouldn't happen for her.

She leads Alex through to the 'cosy' spare room, which Olly used to occupy with his musical instruments and general clutter. Since he left, Kitty has cleared it out; removed the curtains, letting the light flow in, whether that is daylight or the orange glow of the streetlights, and here she paints in perfect silence, just her and her thoughts. There are some pet portraits which she has nearly completed and needs to send on their way, and there is a landscape of the long barrow at night.

"That's gorgeous," Alex says.

"Do you think so?" Kitty can't hide the pleased look on her face.

"Yes, I do! I love the sky."

"It's a work in progress. I want to do a series, in daylight and at night, through the seasons."

"It's a beautiful place," he says.

She nods. "Can I show you this one?" she asks shyly, tugging at my heartstrings as she always has. She turns the canvas to face him and he sees an image of me. Not 'ill me'. Not even seventy-something me, but me as a thirty-three-year-old, heavily pregnant with Kitty. I was sitting on a bench in Cornwall; we'd taken toddler Annie for a winter break down there, and I remember Graham helping her hold our camera still to take a photo of me. This photo is propped up near the painting, and Kitty has been working on it ever since she came back to her flat on New Year's Day.

"That's Ruth?" Alex asks.

Kitty nods confirmation.

"It's beautiful. She's beautiful. Like you and Annie."

Kitty blushes and tuts and shakes her head.

"It's true!" he protests, smiling. "I don't mean it in a slimy way, I promise. Kitty, I'm so sorry about what happened. I should never have kissed you, and I feel awful about it."

"It was both of us," she says, generously.

"No it wasn't. Not really. Look, I haven't come here to tell you what to say or what not to say to Annie. I just wanted to warn you that she and Tom are coming your way, and I – well, I wanted to see you. I've missed you."

"Oh Alex." The tears are back, and Kitty moves towards him, putting her arms around him and her head against his chest, where her tears wet his shirt. This feels right, she realises. He feels like a brother again. She steps back. "And are things OK, with you and Annie, I mean?"

"They are," he says. "I mean, I still irritate her."

"Of course," Kitty smiles.

"Of course," he grins back. "But we're OK."

"Good."

They return to the small living area, and sit companionably, sipping their tea. Kitty puts the TV on and they watch a celebrity antiques programme, soon finding themselves laughing with each other, both pleased to find things feeling normal. When Alex gets up to go, Kitty hugs him again.

"Thanks for coming," she says. "It's been good to see you."

"You too." He kisses the top of her head and goes back towards his car. The lights flash in the darkness as he unlocks it and she watches him climb in, fiddling with his phone – probably messaging Annie, she thinks – then the headlights turn on and he is on his way, slowing down to call goodbye to her. Kitty turns and goes back into the flat, closing the door behind her. She feels better than she has for some time, and she heads into the study to finish those pet portraits before bed. Tonight, she thinks, she'll sleep well.

8

Kitty finds she is grateful to Alex for his warning, as it gives her time to prepare for her brother and sister. She packs the pet portraits she's completed and posts them off in her lunch break. On Thursday and Friday evening, she cleans the flat from top to bottom. It's silly really, because of all the people in all the world, it's her brother and sister who know her best but, while Tom won't give a second thought to what her flat looks like, she wants to present her best side to Annie. Despite everything, she craves her older sister's approval, and she wants Annie to know that she, creative Kitty with barely two pennies to rub together, is more than capable of looking after herself.

It's a defence mechanism, of course. The problem is not really the state of her flat, but what has happened between her and Alex. She allows herself to feel antagonistic towards Annie, imagining her sister's critical eye casting over her small, crammed rooms and messy mini studio; Annie, with her beautifully kept grown-up's house. Kitty feels like she needs to be on the offensive, even though deep down she knows it's her that is in the wrong.

Oh, my girl. My girls, in fact. I want to be there for them, with them; to help them navigate through this. *It's not as bad as you think, Kitty,* I want to say.

This is the biggest challenge of my present situation. I have to accept I can no longer be part of their world, in the way I once was. It's frustrating and almost stifling, and I'm grateful to be able to retreat to the peace and the space of the long barrow, and my friends there, who understand.

Saturday morning comes around and Kitty heads into work as normal. On her return she sees my old car parked up on her street. It gives her a jolt for a moment, as she pictures me getting out, greeting her with a smile and a hug. She shakes the thought away.

Tom, perhaps due to that sixth sense, has insisted on driving Annie, even though her car is nicer and plusher, and superior in every way. Or maybe he just wanted to make sure he got to choose the music and didn't have to put up with Annie's constant driving companion: the dreaded Radio 4.

Either way, they have clearly been watching for their sister because, as she pulls up a couple of spaces behind them, they open their car doors and approach her.

This is it, thinks Kitty. *Best foot forward.*

"What are you doing here?" She does a pretty good job of appearing surprised, I'll give her that. The pleasure at the sight of them is genuine, though.

The daylight is fading and many of the houses along the street have their lights on, some with curtains drawn but others offering tantalising glimpses into the ordinary lives of everyday folk.

No such thing, thinks Kitty. *No ordinary lives, no everyday folk.* Who knows what has happened – is happening – in her neighbours' worlds? What is happening in hers is unimaginable. She hugs Tom, then Annie, and is glad to see that her sister, though not overly enthusiastic in her embrace, is in no way annoyed at her, so presumably the secret is safe. Buried.

"We thought we'd surprise you," Tom says, smiling widely. "Take you out for something to eat, save you cooking. And we haven't seen you in ages!"

Annie flashes a look at Tom. She clearly thinks this is not something to be broached just yet.

"Wow! That's so lovely. Thank you," Kitty says. "I know it's been far too long, I've been crap. I've just had loads of work on, lots of portrait orders to finish..."

It's Tom's turn to shoot a look at Annie now. *Told you so*, he's saying. He has not been too bothered by Kitty's absence. It seems pretty reasonable to him – when she lives and works a good couple of hours away, and she's spent an awful lot of time coming home in these last few months – that she might want to settle back into her own life a bit now.

"But I am so glad to see you both," Kitty says, and it's true. She feels awash with emotion, in fact, at the sight of them, and as they follow her into her flat, although she's still glad that she gave it a good once-over, the sense of having to put up any kind of front just dissipates. She hugs her brother and her sister again.

"Sorry, I must stink of the kennels! I'll have a shower before we go out."

"Don't worry about that," Tom says.

"Well, she might want to," Annie says, which makes Kitty smile. That is the closest Annie can get to being subtle. She definitely thinks Kitty should have a shower and get changed before they go out anywhere.

Kitty is happy to oblige. "I'll put the kettle on, if you want to make a drink while I'm getting ready?"

She notices she'd already put three cups on the side, ready for her siblings' arrival. What was she thinking? That makes it obvious she was expecting them. They don't seem to have noticed, though.

"Go on," says Annie. "I'll make the tea. You go and get ready." She smiles at her little sister, realising how much she's missed her.

My heart glows at the sight of the three of them back together again, and at their clear love and affection for each other. This is one of my proudest achievements in life; not that I can really take credit for it – they are their own people, after all.

In the shower, Kitty almost forgets the whole Alex thing. She sings to herself as she washes her hair, and washes away the grime and the memories of the day's work. It's been a tough one, with a pregnant mixed-breed brought to them, from another rescue who didn't have space for her. The dog is clearly quite young and she's nervous, too. The vet has confirmed she's not far off giving birth as well. It's hard, seeing animals this way, and wondering what they've been through. But better to be part of it and trying to make a difference than to pretend it isn't happening, Kitty thinks. Nevertheless, she's glad to have an evening out with her brother and sister.

"Are you staying over?" she calls through.

"You haven't got space, have you?" Annie asks.

"We can squeeze in. Tom can have the sofa. You can share with me!" Kitty realises there is nothing she'd like more than for them all to have a night together. "Tom can have a drink then as well, and we won't have to worry about rushing back."

"I'm in!" says Tom, full of his usual enthusiasm. It's funny, how much he still looks up to his sisters, and he wants to ask their advice – or he thinks he does – about Cecily.

"Sure," Annie smiles. "Though I won't be drinking. I'm doing dry February."

"Are you?"

"Yes, I did January too. I like it."

"It won't hurt to have a couple tonight," Tom cajoles.

"No, honestly, I feel better than I have in ages. I don't want to ruin that now. But don't let that stop you two. In fact, I can drive Mum's car. We're all on the insurance. I'll drive and then we don't have to worry about taxis. We'll stay over though, Kitty, if that's OK."

"That is more than OK!" says Kitty, rubbing her hair with a towel then taking a glug of the tea Annie's made her. "Brilliant!"

Kitty hasn't been in my car in months. She sniffs the air surreptitiously, trying to see if she can still detect me. She is disappointed to find there is not a slight hint of my perfume. Still, it is strange to sit there, in the passenger seat, and to remember that I'm no longer with them (if only they knew).

"Where to?" Annie asks.

"I know just the place." Kitty directs Annie to the Young Buck, the pub not too far from Meg's kennels. On the way, she tells them about the new rescue case.

"You should have one of the puppies!" Tom says. "It could come to work with you, it'd be perfect."

"It's tempting!" Kitty says. "I think I've got enough on my plate at the moment though."

"Oh?" Annie glances sideways at her sister although in the dark, Kitty's face is only partially lit by the headlights of an oncoming car.

"I just mean with work and all, and I'm –I'm trying to get somewhere with my painting. Not just the portraits. I really want to see if it can go somewhere."

"Like where?" Annie asks, and Kitty bristles. For once, Annie is sensitive enough to realise. "I don't mean that in a negative way. Really, I genuinely want to know what your plans are."

Tom, in the back, relaxes. He soaks up any tension in the family, he always has, which is not much fun for him. He takes the chance to smooth things over now. "I'm curious, too. What are you hoping for?"

"Well, I suppose, to create art that comes from – no, no, you'll laugh at me."

"We won't!" Tom protests. "Look at me, I'm determined to make a living from my music. You don't laugh at me, do you? Do you?" he asks again, hoping that in fact it will make his sisters laugh. He is rewarded.

"Of course we don't," Kitty says. "Or at least not all of the time. No, well, I suppose, I just want to create what comes from within. I know that sounds really vague. I'm working on a series of images of the long barrow. Well, I've nearly finished the first. But I hope to make it a series."

"Really? Will you show us?"

"Yes, of course," Kitty says to Tom then, seeing the pub sign up ahead, she directs Annie to the car park.

"This looks great," says Tom. "And I could murder a beer."

Kitty is pleased to see the approval on Annie's face as they walk in. She knew her sister would like this place. The Young Buck is an old pub, with mismatched furniture and a huge fireplace at its centre. One of the tables by the fire still has a couple of empty glasses and a crisp packet on it but it looks to have been vacated.

"Here, I'll take those to the bar," Kitty says, "you two take the chairs, and I'll get the first round in."

Tom has a pint of pale ale, Kitty has a spiced rum with ginger ale, and Annie has lime and soda.

"Are you sure you can't be tempted to a wine?" Kitty asks, but Annie shakes her head and really, Kitty is pleased her sister's taking a break from drinking – wine had become a bit of a fallback for Annie since I became ill, maybe even before then, so maybe this dry spell is a sign that she is feeling a little better about life. Besides, she certainly looks well on it. Kitty says so.

"Thank you," says Annie, looking almost bashful. Is that a little pink tinge in her cheeks?

"You do look well, sis," says Tom. "You both do," he adds quickly, always keen to be fair.

"You don't have to say that!" Kitty laughs. "I know I look knackered at the moment."

"Are you not sleeping?" Annie asks.

"No, I… I am. I just had a couple of late nights, tidy… finishing those portraits I mentioned, and then last night I stayed up working on the long barrow painting too. Plus work is hard, you know? Physically, and emotionally."

"I hear you, sister," Tom grins.

"Your work must be like that as well, though, Tom.

You're carting people about and I bet you see all sorts of things."

"Yes, I... it is tough actually, sometimes," he says. "Makes me think of Mum."

They all fall quiet at this.

"Sorry," he says, a tear in his eye.

"Don't be sorry," Kitty reaches out and squeezes Tom's hand. "You should tell us things like that. And it's not like we're not all thinking of her most of the time. How's Dad getting on?"

"He's much the same," Annie says. She fights the urge to say, *Why don't you come and see for yourself?* She has been a little bit annoyed with Kitty for keeping her distance lately but, unusually, Alex has had some sanguine advice, and even more unusually, she has listened to him.

"You're all trying to find your own way through this," he said. "And Kitty's life isn't here anymore, is it? So maybe she's trying to find her way in the place where she actually lives and works. And maybe – maybe it's too painful for her to come back here at the moment."

It had made sense to Annie. It was a little bit pathetic, she thought, if her sister couldn't put her own feelings aside and come back to make sure their dad was alright, but she does know that everyone grieves differently. That was something else Alex had said to her, and she had to admit he was right.

"I will come back soon," Kitty says now, as if she's

reading Annie's thoughts. "I can't believe it's been so long, really. I think… it's dark so early, at the end of each day I just want to come in and go to bed, and – actually, I'd quite like to just stay in bed all day, most days. I have to really push myself to keep going sometimes."

"I know what you mean," Tom says.

"I don't," Annie responds, which is no surprise to either of them.

"But you love your work. You pretty much *are* your work!" Tom immediately regrets this. Will it annoy her?

"You're right," Annie says. "I do love it. And it keeps my mind off… other things. I'm lucky. I love what I do. I hope, I really do, that you both get to do what you love. Art and music," she says. It makes her brother and sister smile.

"Thank you, Annie," says Kitty.

The heat from the fire is such that they end up in short sleeves, cheeks flushed, and they decide to eat three courses, with Tom and Kitty sharing a bottle of wine. They talk and laugh, and reminisce, and despite their shared sadness, it feels good. All is as it should be between them again, at least for this one evening.

9

I know what's going on, you see. I am by no means 'all seeing', but when it comes to my family I do have a lot of insight, and I think I know where this is all heading. Kitty is not the only one with a secret.

Back at the flat, Annie puts the kettle on while Tom and Kitty loll about on the settee, pleasantly tipsy but not overly so.

"This is so nice!" Kitty says. "Thanks so much for coming to see me. I think I needed this."

"We all did," says Tom. "Listen, I wanted to ask your advice about something…" He is hoping to bend Kitty's ear first, knowing she's a bit more 'on the ball' emotionally.

"Oh yes?" Sharp-eared Annie doesn't miss a thing. Even standing near the noisy kettle, she catches Tom's words.

"Yes, I… wasn't sure whether to mention this or not, but I've met somebody I like."

"Really, Tom? That's great!" Kitty does her best to push back her childish thought that if Tom gets a girlfriend, she'll be the only single one left.

"Yes, I mean, it's nothing yet. I don't even know if she likes me."

"So who is it?" Annie demands. "Somebody at work? A doctor?" No reason her brother shouldn't aim high in his relationships, she thinks, even if he doesn't in his career.

Tom laughs. "No, not somebody at work. And I don't think many doctors will be looking to a lowly porter for their ideal mate! No. It's somebody you know, actually…"

"Cecily!" Kitty grins. She knows she's right.

"How did you…?"

"I've seen those looks you give her! I'm not stupid. And you do spend a lot of time at the barrow…"

"Yes, but that's to see Mum," he protests, his earnestness reminding his sisters of when he was a little boy.

"I know, of course it is," Kitty soothes.

"Yes, of course." Annie laughs, and so does Kitty. Now Tom himself is reminded of being a little boy; that feeling of his big sisters laughing at him.

"She's not even there most of the time!" he says. "And I do go to see Mum." Frustratingly, he finds himself close to tears.

Kitty sees this and puts her hand on Annie's arm to prevent any further leg-pulling. "Sorry, Tom."

"Yes, sorry," Annie says. "So what are you going to do about it?" Straight to the point as always.

"I… I don't know. That's what I wanted to ask you about. What do you think?"

"I think she's lovely," Kitty says. "And right up your street, Tom. Honestly, I think she looks at you the same way, you know. And I wouldn't say that if I didn't mean it."

"She is nice," Annie says, cautiously, as she carries over three mugs of tea. Kitty makes space for her on the sofa. "And very… you."

"I'm not sure if you're saying that like it's a good thing or a bad thing!" Tom grins, back on safer ground again.

"Tom, you're a catch!" Annie says suddenly. "I mean, you know I think you could be earning more, and be a bit more driven. And smarten up a bit—"

"Alright, alright!"

"But Tom, I honestly think any girl would be lucky to go out with you. And Cecily is kind, and thoughtful, which hopefully means she'd treat you well."

"I agree," says Kitty. "Not about you smartening up, or earning more – I don't think I have a leg to stand on there – but about Cecily being nice, and about you being a catch. I say go for it!"

"Really?" Tom is smiling from ear to ear now. It's nice to see him like this; it's been a while.

"Yes. So – as Annie says, what are you going to do?"

"I don't know. I can't really go loitering around the barrow for her. Although I did see her early on New Year's Day, and we went to watch an owl."

Kitty maintains a poker face, thinking they must have just missed each other. That was a lucky escape. Instead, she smiles. "You see! Perfect for each other! I'm sure Dad must have her number. Why don't you give her a ring?"

"I don't think I should, if she hasn't given me her number herself."

His sisters nod approvingly at this.

"Doesn't she work in a pub as well?" asks Kitty.

"Yes, the Old Man and the Well."

"That's a nice place. Why don't you pop in there sometime, maybe go with a couple of mates? Keep it casual. Have a chat with her, and just see if she fancies a drink sometime… Like the thought's just occurred to you!"

"Seems a bit long-winded," says Annie. "Just go in there and ask her out."

"OK, thanks sisters. You've given me something to think about there. Going to see her in the pub's a good idea, as long as she doesn't just turn me down and I get laughed out of the bar."

"As if that would happen!" smiles Kitty.

Annie's phone starts to ring. "Oh shit, it's Dad!" she says. "I said I'd tell him we'd got here safely."

Kitty sees she has three missed calls from him. Tom has five.

"Hi Dad," says Annie. "I'm sorry, I forgot to message you. We got here and went straight to the pub, more or less. I should have let you know… yes…

and actually we're staying here for the night."

All three of them are too old to be telling their parents their plans, but at the moment it's important for Graham to know that everyone is safe and well. When Annie hangs up, they are more subdued again.

"Was he OK?" asks Kitty.

"Yeah, and a bit embarrassed, I think. But he was worried about us."

"I'll give him a ring tomorrow," says Kitty. "And I will come home soon."

"Good."

"I was thinking," said Tom, "maybe we should go away together – with Dad, I mean... a trip to London or something. The weekend of Mum's birthday...?"

"That's a great idea, Tom," Kitty smiles. "I think Dad would love that."

"I just thought it might be nice for us all to be together. I think it might be a strange day."

"It's not for ages yet!" Annie speaks as she finds, as usual. Kitty shoots her a look. Annie concedes, "But that is a lovely idea."

Annie just doesn't tend to look ahead in that way, or pre-empt events in the way that Tom and Kitty do. Besides, she has a lot on her mind.

Tom wishes that he'd saved the suggestion for another time. The mood has been broken by Graham's phone call, which has brought them all back to earth with a bump. He'd hate to know that, of course; he'd have loved to have seen his three children having such a good time together, but perhaps he's felt a little bit left out as well. Maybe that's what has prompted the excess of phone calls almost as much as the need to know that they are all safe and well.

Now, our daughters and son suddenly begin to feel very tired and when the tea is finished Kitty digs out the sleeping bag and a spare pillow for Tom. She's pleased she'd changed the sheet and covers on her own bed, and once she and Annie have said goodnight to their brother, they go through and slide under the covers.

"Are you alright, Annie?" Kitty asks, just really wanting to know that her sister is getting by.

"Yes. Why?" Annie stiffens.

"No real reason," Kitty assures her. "It's just a hard time, isn't it?"

"Yes."

They are both quiet for a while, each listening to the other breathing.

Then… "Kitty?" Spoken quietly, in case her sister is actually asleep.

"Yes?"

"Can I tell you something?"

"Of course." Kitty's heart is beating rapidly now, although surely she'd already know if Annie knew anything about the kiss. And this isn't how that revelation would start anyway, is it?

Here it comes, I think… the secret only Annie and I know about. The thing I am really quite excited about, and also so sad I am not there to experience.

"The thing is… I think I might be pregnant."

There is a heartbeat's silence.

"Pregnant?"

"Yes." Unsure in the dark, Annie laughs nervously. She has doubts enough about her prospects of being a good mother.

"Oh my god!" Kitty is laughing, but not in a mean way. And she's smiling, Annie can tell.

"You don't think it's a terrible thing?"

"Terrible? No." *Is she crying*? Annie wonders. "I think it's… wonderful. Beautiful, in fact." *She is, she's crying.*

Annie reaches out for her sister, puts her arm around her. *Practice for being a mum*, she thinks, realising she has always felt this protection for Kitty and Tom. Maybe she isn't wholly unprepared. Perhaps she won't be as useless as she's been suspecting.

"Have you done a test?"

"No, not yet."

"Does Alex know?"

"No, not yet."

In truth, Annie hasn't wanted to tell him, which she knows is not the best indicator of a healthy relationship. It's just that right now, it's hers, this baby. This secret. This news. Once he knows, it will be his too, and he'll be so excited. She can just tell. He won't be able to stop going on about it. And right now, she is trying to ease herself into this new, alien situation. Coming to terms with it in her own way. Because it will change everything, she knows that much. Yet, unplanned though this baby is, it does not feel like the end of the world. In fact, it seems a bit like the beginning.

"When are you going to tell him?" Kitty wipes her eyes and her nose. She leans up on her elbow and looks at her sister, trying to find her features in the darkness.

"Soon," Annie says breezily. "When I know for sure."

She doesn't want to be disloyal to Alex; how she feels and what she lets on to the rest of the world do not have to match.

Kitty falls quiet. The two of them lie side by side, on their backs, staring into the soft, blank night.

"What are you thinking?" Annie ventures.

"Oh, I don't know. Loads of things!" Kitty laughs. "I'm thinking how lovely it is that you're going to be a mum–" Annie smiles at this – "and I'm so excited that I'm going to be an aunt. And that your baby; that tiny little being growing inside you has a little bit of Mum inside him or her. You're helping Mum live on."

Annie feels tears running down either side of her face, into her hair. "I won't be able to be like Mum, though. I didn't even think I had a maternal bone in my body. This wasn't planned, you know." She thinks back to New Year's Eve. This baby has to have been a product of what happened between her and Alex then.

She's not the only one thinking of that night. Kitty, having been stunned and delighted by the news, feels

104

even worse now about what happened with Alex. But they agreed to pretend it hadn't happened. And she can't tell Annie now, can she?

"Alex kissed me."

The words are out before she even knew they were coming. She wants to ram them back into her mouth, wind back the seconds.

I wince. *Kitty, what were you thinking?* I mean, it had to come out sometime, I know, but right now? Just when her sister has confided in her the biggest and best news she has had in some time, if not ever?

"What?" It's like the very air turns cold. That gentle, comforting darkness now seems laced with danger. Kitty wants to see her sister's expression but at the same time she dreads it.

"On New Year's Eve." Oh, if only she knew the extra injury that causes. The very same night that Annie and Alex slept together and set this all in motion.

There is silence. Kitty cannot even hear her sister's breath. She ploughs on.

"It was nothing. Something and nothing. And I shouldn't have told you. But I couldn't not. Oh my god, Annie. Oh god. I'm so sorry." She can bear it no longer and she pulls the cord above the headboard, flooding the room with light. She sees her sister, eyes tightly closed. "Annie." Kitty reaches a hand out and touches her sister's shoulder. It is hard; unyielding.

"He kissed you?" Annie hisses, eyes still closed tight.

"Yes. Well. Just for a moment. And I didn't stop him,

so I'm as much to blame." Kitty is scrabbling now, feeling terrible for Alex. Terrible for Annie. Wishing she'd just kept to the plan she and Alex had agreed and kept her stupid mouth shut. But she can't go back now, and the secret is out.

Annie turns her back on her. "Let's get some sleep."

Kitty, ever the younger sister, obliges by pulling the light cord again and they sink into darkness once more. But where before there was secrecy and camaraderie; excitement and delight, now hurt, betrayal, and fear mingle. There is no way either of my girls is getting much sleep tonight.

10

The journey back home is awkward. Tom feels awkward, at least, although he is not quite sure why. Annie is simply lost in a world of her own.

"What happened?" Tom had asked Kitty in the kitchen.

"I can't say," Kitty tells him, her eyes on his. "Not yet. I think maybe you should ask Annie."

She is desperate that her brother shouldn't hate her, but she feels it's only right that he gets Annie's side of the story first. Kitty is not the one who has been wronged, after all. She does not deserve to get in there first and perhaps gain Tom's understanding, or even sympathy.

She had lain in bed feeling dehydrated and also desperate for the toilet, but not sure whether Annie was asleep, and not wishing to disturb her if she was. When the night was finally over, and daylight began to impinge on the morning, she could wait no longer.

"Just going to the loo," she whispered, to no response from Annie. Perhaps she actually had fallen asleep. But no, when Kitty got back into her bedroom,

Annie was already dressed, rummaging around her handbag.

"Are you OK?" Kitty asked – one of the most futile questions known to man.

"What do you think?" Annie asked, staring at her sister.

"Never felt better?" Kitty ventured a little joke, all the while wondering what she was doing. It went down pretty much as well as she might have expected. "Sorry. You must hate me, Annie."

"Hate you? No. Alex? Maybe."

"But we were both…"

"He kissed you, you said so. You didn't kiss him."

"No, but…"

"What? Did it go further?" Annie looked shocked, disgusted, and maybe even a little fearful at the thought.

"Did it…? No, of course not!" Kitty knew she did not one hundred per cent discourage Alex, but she was experiencing a cowardly sense of relief that her sister was not actually angry at her.

"Then why should I hate you? No. I'm glad you told me."

Say something, Kitty, I thought. I actually felt sorry for Alex, having no idea of what is coming his way. She did speak, but only to say, "What are you going to do?"

She let it slide. Allowing Alex to take full responsibility for what happened.

It was *him who kissed me*, Kitty justified to herself, all the while knowing that, if she is honest, she didn't immediately pull away.

By the time Tom asked her what was going on, she had begun to feel that she should definitely be taking some of the blame. That with a bit of thinking time, maybe Annie would start to feel differently about things; and certainly it was her sister who should get their brother's ear, not her.

Annie does not take the chance, though. She feels scalded by the idea that her husband has kissed her sister. She is embarrassed, even, and what Kitty cannot know is that this has compounded what she has always suspected; that she, Annie, is a lesser person than her younger sister. Friendly, funny, creative, caring Kitty, who has always had so many friends, and such an upbeat way about her. It's not Kitty's fault that she's an easier person than Annie, and more fun to be around – any more than it is her fault that Alex kissed her. Annie feels this keenly, but it doesn't make her feel any better about herself.

"You coming in to see Dad?" Tom asks as they pull up on the drive.

"No, I'd better get… home," Annie says. "Tell him I'll call him later."

"OK." Tom is disappointed. Deflated. He'd enjoyed last night so much, and he'd lain on Kitty's sofa buoyed up with thoughts of Cecily, imagining telling her about his great idea for this family weekend away to celebrate my birthday. The atmosphere this morning had quickly killed those vibes.

He'd watched Annie get into her car and drive away then he'd gone into the house, where at least he got an enthusiastic welcome from Mavis.

"Hi son," Graham said, stirring a steaming pot on the stove. "I'm making a chilli."

"Great, Dad." Tom said, grateful for Graham's commitment to keeping busy and productive.

Take away any member of a family and it is thrown into turmoil. There is a balance, and a way of being, which is so normal it is never even noticed, and it is taken for granted, until it is no longer. It's like removing a leg from a table and it's very difficult to see how or if stability can be achieved again, or what that stability might look like.

Tom and Graham, I am proud to say, are finding a way to make it work and, although it is far from easy, my absence now is drawing them closer. That, I am thankful for; particularly in the face of the oncoming storm.

11

Alex is a bag of nerves. He feels sick. Kitty, of course, had warned him that she'd told Annie. It was the least she could do, she thought guiltily.

His wife will be home soon, he supposes – unless she decides to stay out longer, to punish him. What should he do? He can't go out; he can't risk not being here when she gets back, although the cowardly side of him would like nothing more than to avoid the inevitable altercation. For all his faults, though, Alex is not a coward. Not really. And he knows this has to happen sometime. Also, for all his agitation and fear, he is aware of a slight sense of relief. He is no more a liar than a coward, and although he and Kitty had agreed to pretend nothing had happened between them, there has been a low-lying feeling of guilt trickling away deep within him. In fact, he had felt particularly bad when he'd returned from his visit to her earlier in the week, when he'd got in to find that Annie had been busy making dinner for them both. She had just assumed he was working late that night and unusually she seemed quite pleased to see him.

Over the years, Alex has become accustomed to a cursory hello from Annie; there is rarely a kiss, and never a hug. It's just who she is, he has come to realise, and not a reflection of their relationship – at least he hopes not. Typical, then, that on the evening of the day he's paid a secret visit to his wife's sister, to discuss the illicit kiss they had shared, and furthermore to betray Annie's trust by pre-warning Kitty of what was supposed to be a surprise visit – he returned home to a smile, a cold beer in the fridge, and a really pretty tasty lasagne, all things considered.

Ever since Kitty rang him this morning, Alex has been playing and replaying different scenarios and conversations in his mind. He tries out different tacks: defensive ("I didn't plan it, and it didn't mean anything anyway. Just a stupid slip-up. I wasn't thinking. Really, it was barely a kiss."); offensive ("You'd been cold to me all evening, when all I was trying to do was look after you. I never know where I stand with you. At least Kitty's nice to me."); blaming Kitty ("She was upset, and sitting in her room with the door open. I just wanted to comfort her…")

Pathetic, all of it, and he knows it. Because if he's honest, he knows there is no defence – no excuse. If Annie is cold to him (and she is), it doesn't follow that he should kiss her sister. If he 'accidentally' kissed Kitty, then he must be even more stupid than Annie normally thinks he is. And if he tries to insinuate that Kitty is to blame, well, that's just pretty despicable really. His younger, grief-stricken sister-in-law. An image of Kitty's face comes to him; her look of horror immediately after they had kissed, and then the worry that had crossed her features when he'd seen her earlier this week. No, he will not – cannot – even think of trying to blame her.

All he can do is wait.

At the sound of the front door, he jumps. He switches off the TV. Takes a deep breath. Walks into the hallway.

The familiarity of Annie surprises him, somehow; he's built this encounter up to such an extent that it's almost like he's been expecting her to have changed significantly in the short time she's been away. But no, here she is, in her usual coat, and her everyday boots; there is even the scent of her perfume that he knows so well. The only thing that is really different is the scowl on her face.

He plays it well; he keeps his counsel, and he waits for her to speak.

She pulls off her boots, and then she looks up.

"How could you?" she asks, glaring at him.

They both understand that there is no need to specify to what she refers.

"I'm sorry," he says, and he can feel the tears pushing at the backs of his eyes, but he keeps the floodgates in place. There is no sympathy for him here, and nor should there be.

"*Sorry*?" she sneers. "Is that the best you can do?" She marches into the kitchen, puts the kettle on, and then she sits heavily on one of the stools at the breakfast bar. She looks worn out, Alex thinks, and he wants nothing more than to go to her and put his arms around her, but he has no doubt that she will not want to be comforted by him. Not now, and maybe never again. The thought is like a punch in the guts. How could he have been so stupid? So fucking, fucking stupid. And ridiculous. Never all that high on self-esteem, Alex thinks now that he probably actually hates himself.

"I don't know what else to say. Honestly. If I could do anything to make things different, I would. It should never have happened."

"What should never have happened?"

"You know."

"Yes. I do. But I want to hear you say it."

"The kiss," he mumbles... nearly stumbles on his words. His eyes are on the kitchen floor but then, *No*, he thinks. *I need to do this properly. This is my wife. She deserves better from me.*

"I should not have kissed your sister." Alex looks Annie in the eye. I've never been so proud of him.

"She's got a name." Oh she's a hard one, Annie, or she can be when she needs to be. "Say it."

"Kitty," he says, and he's still looking at her. He speaks slowly; clearly: "I should not have kissed Kitty."

"No. You shouldn't."

114

He keeps quiet now. Awaits his fate.

"How could you, Alex? How could you take advantage of her like that? She's heartbroken – we all are – about Mum, and it was our first Christmas, first New Year's, without her. Not to mention Olly. That twat she was living with. In six months she's lost her mum and her boyfriend, and then you come along and you fucking kiss her. Her own brother-in-law! Taking advantage of her when she's vulnerable. Disgusting." Annie gets down from the stool and throws a teabag into a cup, sloshing in the hot water from the kettle with just enough care to avoid splashing herself.

She does not offer him a cup, Alex notices, but it's not that which hurts him. It's the realisation that her anger is all about Kitty. Nothing that Annie has said to him suggests that she is at all bothered about herself. There is no jealousy. Nothing to imply that there is any hurt on her own behalf. Confirming to him, as he has long suspected, that his wife no longer loves him; if she ever did.

What Alex has not seen are Annie's tears. They have all been shed, for the time being at least. Silently in Kitty's bed, and loudly as she drove away from our family home after Tom had gone inside. She could not go home in such a state, and so Annie came to the long barrow. She needed some time, and some space, to think, and to let these difficult, confusing feelings find their feet.

She walked purposefully up the long path to the barrow, grateful she'd had her wellies in the boot of her car. It means she can tread meaningfully through the small troughs where the standing water has gathered, and there is something satisfying in that – the crunch of the stones, and the splash of the cold, brown water. She experiences a flashback to an image of her and Kitty, playing in the puddles in our back garden one rainy day. I remember that day, too. We'd been stuck inside, with Tom a tiny baby, and the girls were getting at each other. I'd sent them outside in their raincoats and wellies – Annie's were red and Kitty's yellow. The image of those boots is vivid now, in our memories: bold, vibrant colour against a grey, cloudy day. It provokes a gulp of sorrow from Annie, who thinks how simple life used to be. Would she go back, if she could? To childhood? To a time before all her incredible achievements; her career that she's so proud of, and her nice house and car? Without a doubt, she thinks, she'd go back. Retreat into a safe, warm world where she had no responsibilities; no decisions more complex than which book to read, or which colour socks to put on.

Annie remembered what we had done later that same day, prompting my own reminiscence. I'd packed us all into my little car – me, Annie, Kitty and

Tom. It had been a long old day, and we were all going a bit stir-crazy. With a brainwave, I'd put the girls' tea into their school lunchboxes, and driven us to a nearby lake, where we could sit in the car close to the water and watch the ducks and the geese. I took the keys from the ignition and I let the girls sit in the front seats so that they had a better view for their picnic, while I sat in the back and fed Tom.

At Kitty's encouragement, Annie set the windscreen wipers going, and I remember so vividly that *squeak, squeak* sound, while the rain pattered on the roof, and ran down the steamed-up windows. Almost by magic, when the girls were slurping the last of their milkshake cartons, the rain slowed, and the sun shone torch-like beams through the clouds. We got out of the car, and I remember feeling elated by the sense of freedom, and the smiles on the girls' faces, as they emerged, stretching and bouncing off each other with glee.

Yes, Annie, I thought, *I know exactly why you would want to go back to that.*

In her sadness and confusion, all she wanted to do was retreat. But through her memory and mine, I knew as well that she was missing something; something which I hope she will find out soon for herself. For all her child's joy at playing with her little sister; for all the security of having me, or Graham, there to take charge, make decisions... she has not yet felt the happiness I experienced that day, and countless other days, as I held Tom close to me, and watched my daughters smiling and laughing in the early evening sunshine. Yes, it is hard being a grown-up, and often disappointing, or anxiety-inducing, but I would not have changed anything if it meant missing out on moments like that.

When Annie reached the long barrow this afternoon, she was exhausted. She punched in the numbers on the lock and she walked in. She is not one for greetings; she does not feel the need to speak aloud. She just appreciates the sacred, safe space, its clever design, and the isolation it offers from the outside world. Today, she did not even light a candle; there was enough daylight from the doorway to mean she could see where she was. She could see the stained-glass niche cover, and she touched it briefly, before sitting heavily on the stone seat. Rather than letting herself relax, she sat hunched and stiff, her thoughts and feelings a whirlwind within her. Alex… Kitty… the previous evening with her brother and sister… sleeping with Alex on New Year's Eve. That must have been right after he had kissed her sister. The thought disgusted her. Absolutely disgusted her.

All I could do was be with her. Try somehow, any way I could, to calm her, and to let her breathe. Through that slowing of her breath, I hoped, she would begin to gather herself together, and reduce the speed of her train of thought.

I found the rhythm of her breath. Her heartbeat. I

inhaled, slowly. Nothing. I tried again, my eyes on Annie's face, her eyes closed. She blinked them open, like she felt something. Then she took a deep, involuntary breath. Rolled her shoulders back and gently moved her head from side to side, as she does in her Pilates class. It was working! I inhaled, slowly, again, exhaling towards her. She pushed her head slowly backwards, so her chin pointed up. Then loosened her neck from left to right once more. And then, she stood. Still without a candle, she moved off into the darkness of the corridor and through into the second chamber. A sliver of light fell from the doorway there but the majority of the space was in darkness. Not freaked out or silly in any way, my brave, strong Annie walked around the circumference, trailing her fingers around the wall, feeling the stones and the cracks and the crevices, closing her eyes and feeling her way for a while, listening to each of her footsteps. At the doorway, she stopped. Looked at the vivid colours and the way the air in front of the glass lit up. There was a misty quality right there, but Annie could not bring herself to think it would be anything other than a natural phenomenon. Something to do with the heat of the air inside the barrow opposed to the temperature of the stone, and the floor, and the day outside. She could be right – but she wasn't. For all around her were spirits. Not just me, but all of us who reside within the barrow.

There are times in life when people need extra

strength and they find it, drawing it from they don't know where. But I know, and now you do too. And Annie walked through this gentle mist towards the colours of the door, reaching out one hand to touch them. She saw yellow, and red, like the wellies she and her sister used to wear. And her other hand touched her stomach, feeling the reality and truth of her situation.

By the time she left the long barrow, she knew exactly what she had to do.

12

I'm aware it seems like I have not been paying much attention to Graham and that all my focus is on my children's lives; which, to be fair, is where all the action is. But I'm aware of him, my husband, all the time. And I am overwhelmed occasionally by the need to protect him, and his privacy; even as I spill the details of my children's private lives.

You know he keeps himself occupied, and that is how he gets through the days. It's the nights that fill him with cold terror. Even with faithful Mavis by his side, he's alone. He's lonely, in a way he could never have imagined. These times, I lie with him – with them – and just try to convey somehow that I am still with him. But even if he knew, I suspect it would be small comfort. I am not there in the sense that I have been these past thirty-odd years. There is no solid physical presence in the bed next to him; no reassuring snoring or stealing of covers. Nobody with whom to discuss his fears about the children, or what to do about a school reunion he has been invited to. He can't even think about such a thing without his stomach clenching hard, nearly doubling him over. The concept of social gatherings, with people he doesn't know – or at least hasn't known for decades – without me by his side is enough to send him spinning into panic. And so the invitation remains unanswered. His concerns about Kitty, and Annie, are pushed to one side. Only Tom seems to be coping, thinks Graham, although he knows that really it isn't any easier for our youngest than for anyone else. It can't be. But Tom is steady, reliable, and somehow looks beyond the immediate. In a very strange way, this airiness keeps him grounded.

His daughters are a mystery to him at the moment; even Annie, who is there but not there. She visits as often as she did before, coming for tea a couple of times a week. Alex's absence has been noted, although Annie says that he's just very busy with work. And to be honest, Graham doesn't mind at all. He's glad to have his daughter there alone, and to sit with her and Tom if he's not on shift or out with his friends. So Graham doesn't push too hard at this little blister of doubt about the real reason for Alex not being there.

Kitty, on the other hand, has become very definitely distant. It had to happen, Graham supposes. Her home and her work are nearly two hours away. She's busy at the kennels and, she tells him, pushing her art as well.

"Don't burn the candle at both ends," he has cautioned her.

"But Dad, if I don't do this now, how will I ever get anywhere? I'm young, and I'm single, I don't have kids… I can work late and it doesn't bother anyone."

But don't let it be everything, Graham thought, but he didn't say this. He has to let her find her own way and maybe losing herself in her art is her way of dealing with grief.

God knows, Ruth, he speaks to me in his head. *It's not like I'm an expert.* They are all just finding their own way, he supposes, but still, he is so grateful for Tom's company, knowing that once each night finally closes, and he can leave the confines of his room, as long as Tom is home there will be somebody real and solid and living to talk to.

"Coffee, Dad?" Tom asks cheerfully.

"Yes please, son." Graham feels himself flood with life once he's in the kitchen, and imagines he is being coloured in, from top to toe, like a black-and-white photo being treated with colour. It's not like he misses me any less, but in the kitchen the radio is on, and there is bread in the toaster. The lights are on, and somebody is home.

"Toast?"

"No, you sort yourself out, I'll get something in a bit, thanks." First thing in the morning is when his appetite is at its lowest ebb. "What are your plans today?"

"Got to dash soon, for work."

"And then, are you coming home?" Graham tries not to sound too hopeful.

"Yes, I think so... well, maybe the pub..."

"Sure, of course. You're young. You want to be with your mates." *I hope that doesn't sound too pathetic,* Graham thinks.

"Well, actually, Dad, I was wondering if you fancied coming with me?"

Graham's heart leaps. *Definitely pathetic,* he thinks. "Really?"

"Yes, I... well, I was thinking about going to the Old Man and the Well."

"Oh yes?" Graham smiles despite himself. He knows who works there.

"Yeah, well, I was... tell me if you think this sounds daft. I was thinking we could get something to eat there anyway but also..." Tom's gaze is cast down towards the counter and he's twiddling his fingers. Graham tries to hide his smile but Tom looks so like the eight-year-old he used to be.

"Yes?"

"I was thinking I might... I dunno... I might ask Cecily out. Do you think that's stupid?" Tom looks Graham in the eye at last.

"Stupid? No! Why would I think that?"

"Well, I don't know really. She might say no."

"She might. But if you don't ask, you won't know."

"I knew you'd say that."

"She's a nice lass, Cecily. And she'd be mad to say no."

"Think you might be a bit biased though, Dad!" Tom grins.

"Maybe a little bit."

"So shall we?"

"What? Go to the pub? Yes. I'd love to."

"Great! Thanks, Dad. And I'm not just asking you just because I want to go and ask Cecily out."

"I know son, but I'll be honoured to be your wing man." Graham laughs. Tom does, too. In contrast to all the angst between the women of our family, seeing this relationship develop is a real joy.

When Tom gets home from work, he showers and shaves and changes, then changes again, into some comfortable jeans and a t-shirt with a khaki jacket over the top. He doesn't want to overthink this. He needs to be himself. Otherwise, assuming he gets over the first hurdle and actually manages to ask Cecily out – and assuming she says yes – they're beginning under false pretences. No, Tom thinks, if she's going to go out with him, it needs to be the real thing.

Graham drives, and Tom sweats in the passenger seat, wondering if he can really do this. He considers that he has never really 'asked someone out' before, or at least not since he was about thirteen. Things have just developed with girls; he has a large group of friends, most of them sociable and gregarious so that there are almost always new people coming along to nights out. On occasion, Tom has hit it off with a friend of a friend – or else a friendship has developed with a girl first and a romantic relationship has grown out of that. Now, he thinks, as the only time he sees Cecily is at the long barrow, he's going to have to make a little bit of effort to push this on; see if she might just be interested in him too.

"Come on then," Graham smiles at our boy before they get out of the car, and as they approach the pub entrance he murmurs, "Good luck, son."

Tom just flashes him a nervous smile.

They walk into the dark interior of the pub, where a fire crackles in the hearth, though it's actually a fairly mild day. We are on the home strait to spring now.

Tom's face and shoulders droop as he looks around. She's not here. There is just an older woman, and a young man, serving behind the bar.

"She might be out back," Graham says quietly, but Tom looks at him, enraged. He should never have invited his dad along to ask a girl out. What was he thinking? And now she's not here anyway, but his dad's being so bloody obvious, and then…

"Hello!" She appears behind them, taking them both unawares. "How lovely to see you," she smiles. Cecily is carrying a couple of empty glasses, one with an empty crisp packet folded neatly inside. She raises them up slightly. "It's been so nice out there, we had a couple sitting at one of the tables this afternoon. I don't blame them. It's not exactly warm, but it's so sunny."

"Hi," Tom says, aware of his dad's eyes on him. He tries to ignore this, and picks up the thread of conversation. "I know, it's been a beautiful day. Spring's nearly here."

Oh my god, how old am I? he berates himself. *And why are we talking about the weather?*

"We've just popped in for a bite to eat," he says.

"Great," she smiles. "If you get yourselves sorted for drinks, I'll bring over a menu for you."

"Thanks, love," says Graham warmly.

Urgh. Love? thinks Tom. "Thanks Cecily," he says.

"She's a nice girl," Graham says quietly once they're seated with their drinks and Cecily has brought their menus, as promised.

Tom stops himself from emitting a teenage *Da-ad.*

"Young lady," Graham corrects himself. "Or is it young woman? Your sisters would kill me."

I could kill you myself at the moment, thinks Tom, but he knows he's being unfair. He's just on edge, wondering what he's doing. Shouldn't he just have sent her a WhatsApp or something? But he's here now, and he'll have to make the best of it.

It feels extra awkward though, her waiting on their table, especially when he wishes that it was her sitting with him instead – no offence to Graham.

In time, he relaxes, aided by his second pint of pale ale.

Graham has been asking him about work, and Tom's been doing his best not to feel as though he needs to read between the lines. He knows Graham doesn't really approve of his job; actually, it's not the job as such – Graham knows full well that it's a fine job and a very important one – but the fact that Tom, educated to degree-level, is not getting the benefit of his education, nor getting any closer to paying off his student debt.

Tom knows all this and he does understand, really. He knows that his dad and I grew up with very little, and that he and his sisters have reaped the benefits of our hard work. Graham was the first person in his family to go to university. He worked long hours and sacrificed time at home in return for promotions and career success. In my family, I was pushing the boundaries as a woman wanting qualifications and a career. In return, we have both enjoyed the satisfaction of rewarding jobs, as well as the financial benefits. A nice, secure home. Meals out. Annual holidays, often abroad. The children have received these things as a given, and this has enabled them to feel more free, to choose what they want to do with their lives. Really, I suppose, that's a good thing. Kitty can follow her passion in art, giving it a go, knowing that she does have a safety net to fall back into if she needs to. She is very lucky in this respect. But isn't that what we want for them, really? Life shouldn't have to be all about earning money, although I appreciate that for many people it has to be.

"I'm thinking of getting a band together," Tom says

airily now, although this idea has really only been floating around his head from time to time. He just can't help pushing it with Graham sometimes.

"Oh yes?" I feel my heart squeeze at Graham's response. He's lost his will to fight in this respect. He hasn't the energy to try and push Tom, and besides, his views are changing. Now that he knows for sure that bad things don't only happen to other people, he's beginning to see life from a different vantage point. Now that he is desperately sad, he is beginning to recognise the value of happiness, and that this is not something entirely dependent on a 'good' career, or a nice house, or meals out, or holidays (though he won't see our children go without any of these things – lucky them).

"Yes," Tom says. "I like what Kitty's doing; following her heart. If she doesn't push her art then she'll never know what she might have achieved. I feel the same about music."

"OK," Graham says kindly. "Well it has to happen for some people, I suppose." He's no musician and doesn't really know if Tom is any good but, like I say, he's had the fight knocked out of him.

"Exactly!" It wasn't the response Tom was expecting, but he's gratified. It lifts him, and before he knows it, he's standing up. "Drink?" he asks Graham.

"No, I'm fine thanks." Graham lifts his half-full glass of lemonade.

Tom turns and walks to the bar. He's already clocked that Cecily is serving. She pulls him a pint and as she puts it on the bar he says, "I'd like to buy you a drink one day. If you'd like me to, I mean," he blushes as his confidence suddenly falters. "On a date," he clarifies.

Cecily smiles. "I would like that, yes."

"Really?"

She laughs. "Really."

"That's great. Then is it OK if I get your number off Dad, and give you a ring?"

"Of course!" She is impressed that he's asking, and hasn't just assumed. Tom has a lot to thank his sisters for.

"That's great," he says again, and picks up his pint.

"I'll put that on the tab, shall I?"

"Oh, er, yes," Tom smiles at her. "Please."

"No problem." She returns his smile.

Graham, watching the exchange, can't help grinning to himself. *If only you were here to see this, Ruth*, he thinks.

If only you knew that I am.

13

While Tom and Cecily speak a few times on the phone, and begin to message each other regularly (and when they're not sending messages they are checking to see if they've received any, hearts flipping at the sight of each other's names on their respective screens), my eldest daughter and her husband are living around each other. I wouldn't say they are living with each other, even though they share the same space. They are working a lot of different hours; Annie keeps track of Alex's plans, and makes sure that hers don't match, and they are eating at different times.

On weekends, Annie spends a lot of time at our house, and she doesn't ask Alex to come with her. Graham has noticed. Tom has noticed. They are both also aware that, while they see Annie more and more, Kitty has still not been back home, but her birthday is coming soon.

"Should I ask her if she's coming back?" Graham says to Annie and Tom at lunch one weekend.

"You could do," Tom says, keeping a careful eye on Annie but she maintains a straight face. What is going on with his sisters?

"But she might just want this one to pass by without a fuss," Annie says. "If you think about last year, when Mum was here…" She still can't quite speak about it all without her emotions getting the better of her. The truth is, Kitty's birthday last year was a difficult day. She and Olly came home, and Annie and Alex came over. We had a big lunch and had planned to go for a walk but I had felt shattered and even as we were setting out, I knew I had to acknowledge it.

"I'm too tired," I'd said to Graham, not wanting to worry the kids, but seeing the panic etch itself quickly across his face. "I'm OK," I reassured him. "I just don't think I'm up to a walk."

"Hang on!" Graham had called ahead, where Annie, Kitty and Tom were walking together, Olly and Alex further on still.

I handed Mavis's lead to Kitty. "Could you take her? I think I need to just go and rest this afternoon. I'm sorry."

Her eyes had immediately filled with tears as she accepted the lead. I could see she was annoyed at herself for this. Just beyond her, Tom and Annie were also looking at me and I could see they were both doing their best not to appear worried.

"Don't fret," I'd squeezed Kitty's arm and looked to the other two as well, pasting on a smile. "It doesn't mean anything. I just will feel like this sometimes." As if I knew any better than the rest of them what it would be like but, in my role as Mum, I had to seem like I did. I had to reassure them all.

"OK," she said, rolling her shoulders back, pushing her chin up. "Don't worry, I've got Mavis. You go back and relax and then we can enjoy the evening."

"Thanks, love," I'd kissed her cheek. "Enjoy your walk."

"I'll come back with you," said Graham.

"You don't have to do that."

"No, I know, but I've got things to do in the garden. I'll only hold the youngsters back, anyway."

We both knew that he wanted to be with me, and make sure I was OK, but we were stepping carefully around this thought, and we continued in that vein for as long as we could.

Now it's Annie and Alex stepping carefully, neither wanting to put a foot wrong. Alex is on thin ice, he realises, but Annie has her own reasons for feeling guilty. She's done the test, and she knows for definite that she's pregnant. Nearly ten weeks pregnant, to be precise. Yet she hasn't told Alex.

So while he's obsessing over the kiss, and whether or not she hates him and will ever forgive him, she's considering her situation, and whether or not to tell him. She's even wondered if she should even keep it. The thought of being a mother terrifies her. But, although she would never admit this to anyone because this is just not how Annie's mind normally works, she has an incredibly strong sense that this is her destiny and that, through her baby, she will be helping to keep a little part of me alive. The kiss barely enters Annie's head, if she's honest, but that in itself is further proof to her that the relationship is not what it should be. The real problem is what to do about this.

Kitty has been in touch a number of times, and Annie responds to WhatsApp messages, but she does not instigate them.

Can we talk? Kitty has asked.

Yes but not yet. Annie really just doesn't feel ready for it, and has other things on her mind, but to Kitty this means her sister hates her.

I'm so sorry.

I know. This is as close as Annie gets to reassurance, but Kitty did not read it that way. Her shoulders slumped when she read this and saw that nothing more was forthcoming.

She messaged Tom: **Has Annie spoken to you?**

No. What about? Is everything OK? He knows something is up but has no idea what it could be.

Everything's fine, Kitty responded unconvincingly.

Tom hadn't even bothered to answer. He was reminded of his childhood, when he regularly felt left out of his older sisters' world. Well, whatever it was that was going on, they'd have to sort it out themselves. He had enough to worry about.

Except, he's a peacemaker, and he – like me – finds it very hard to let things be, unless he knows everything is alright. It is clear that everything is not and, after the lunch with Graham when he'd mentioned asking Kitty back for her birthday, Tom asks Annie outright. They are in the kitchen, stacking the dishwasher.

"What's going on, Annie?"

"What do you mean?"

"With you. And Kitty. And you and Alex." He sees her wince slightly but she quickly recovers her composure.

"I don't know what you mean."

"Well, OK." Tom thinks for a moment. He can talk to Kitty far more easily than Annie, but Kitty has been giving nothing away. Besides, Kitty hasn't been back, so she will have no idea that there is a problem with Alex and Annie (if only he knew). "But it's a bit weird, that Alex doesn't come round anymore."

"He's working a lot," she says, her face turned towards the dishwasher.

"Every weekend?"

"No." Her classic defensive posture as she straightens herself up. "But he needs a break as well."

"And what about Kitty?"

"What about her?"

"I don't know." Tom is losing his nerve. He pushes himself on. "But I feel like something happened, when we went to see her. One minute everything was great, and then we were just leaving, and you barely said bye to her, and you hardly spoke on the way home..."

"Don't worry, Tom. Nothing's going on."

"OK. So let's get Kitty back for her birthday. It'll make Dad feel better." He wants to see how she'll react if he pushes this idea.

"Fine."

"Great. Can you ask her, then?"

"Sure." Backed into a corner, Annie doesn't want to give anything away. "I'll message her later."

"Why don't you phone her?"

"OK, Tom. I'll phone her. Later." She takes a cloth from the sink and starts to wipe down a work surface. Not quite satisfied, but understanding this is the end of the conversation, Tom sets the dishwasher off and then wanders away to his room, to message Cecily. They are planning to go out on Wednesday evening, and he's beginning to feel nervous. He pictures the date, and how it would be if things went well. Would he invite her over to celebrate Kitty's birthday? Or would that be too soon – and too weird, given the apparent state of things between his sisters, and also between Annie and her husband?

He finds a wave of emotion washes over him, taking him by surprise. He's so happy that he's got a date with Cecily but it feels like another step away from me. And with all of this going on with Annie and Alex, and Annie and Kitty (surely it can't be a coincidence that Annie is the common factor here, he thinks – unfairly, as it happens), he doesn't know what to do. *Mum*, he thinks. *Mum, I miss you so much.* And oh, that gets me. I love that he thinks I'd know what to do; and

136

somehow, I would have probably tried to find a way forward through it all, but really I would have been making it up, like everyone else does.

Tom, I want to say, *you're doing wonderfully. And you must take these steps on with life. We talked about this.*

If only he knew I could see him, and how proud I am of him. How much I want him to forge ahead and enjoy every last drop of his life.

Because I miss things, about that life. Silly little things like fresh coffee, and crumpets with butter melted all the way through. Bigger things, like a lazy Sunday afternoon watching a film, or a sunny Saturday in late winter, sowing seeds and looking forward to seeing them grow. A summer day, sculling on my back in the sea, watching clouds drift by overhead. Laughing hard with friends. Bigger still; I miss the warmth of human contact. A hug. A held hand. A kiss. The familiar smell of family.

Enjoy it all, Tom, I think. *Be good and strong and support your sisters and your dad as you always do, but take some of this for yourself. Enjoy it, because soon enough it will be gone.*

Meanwhile, Annie wipes the worktops clean and considers what she'll say to her sister. She does actually want to speak to her, she finds, and has been surprised that Kitty that hasn't asked her any more about the pregnancy, but then she's not been exactly forthcoming in her communications. Annie realises she has missed her sister, and she really does need to speak to somebody. Besides – a thought passes through her mind – maybe there really is something between Alex and Kitty? That might solve one of her problems. *Don't be ridiculous*, she tells herself, and dismisses this idea as soon as it's occurred.

14

Kitty is busy mopping down the hard floor of the corridor outside the kennels when she feels her phone vibrating. Expecting the usual unsolicited sales call, she checks the screen, only to see it's her sister.

She stands straight, leaning the mop against her side and pushing a strand of hair out of her eyes.

"Annie?"

"Hi." It's hard to read anything into this one syllable, delivered flatly, but then Annie is not exactly one for extravagant displays of affection or excitement anyway.

"Are you... alright?" Kitty asks. She is longing to ask about the potential pregnancy but just can't bring herself to.

"I'm fine thank you. How are you?" Oh, the politeness is a killer.

"I'm OK," Kitty decides the only thing to do is to brush over the awkwardness. "In fact, I'm mid-mop, so I'm grateful you've called now."

"I can phone back at a better time...?"

"No, no. Don't do that! I mean it, I'm grateful for a break."

"OK. Good. Well, I wanted to know if you're coming back for your birthday."

"I don't know, to be honest. I hadn't really thought about it yet." This is not quite true. She and Meg have hatched a plan to go to the quiz at the Young Buck. It may not be very wild but it should be fun.

"In that case, can you come back home for it please? Dad misses you, and Tom, and…" she can't bring herself to say it but assumes Kitty will read into this that she misses her too. In fact, Kitty takes the very opposite meaning and her stomach drops.

"Oh, erm, I mean, it's on a Saturday so…"

"Exactly. It's on a weekend, and you could come over after work, couldn't you?"

"I…"

"Come on, Kitty. You haven't been back in ages."

"I wouldn't have thought you'd want me to."

Annie snorts. "Don't be ridiculous. Of course I want you to."

"You mean, it's not just Tom and Dad who've missed me?" Kitty allows herself a small, hopeful smile.

"No, no, that's not what I said, was it?"

"It kind of was."

"Well, I'm sorry then. I would like to see you."

"Will Alex be there?" Kitty winces as she says this.

"I… don't know. I'm not sure. I thought maybe it would be nice if it was just me, you, Tom and Dad."

"That would be nice." Kitty relaxes a little.

"Although Tom might want to bring Cecily."

"Cecily? You mean…?"

"Yes!" Annie is smiling now. "They're going on a date on Wednesday."

"Oh, that's really good."

"It is, isn't it? I didn't know if he'd have told you."

"No, I'm afraid I've not been a very good sister to him, or you, lately. But I've thought about you all the time, I really have."

"And I've been thinking about you."

I feel myself relax as my girls do the same. They've needed to have this conversation but have both been too obstinate, or possibly too scared, to make the first move.

"So, I wanted to ask…" Kitty says.

"Yes?" Annie may have softened but still won't make this easy. Besides, she needs to know for sure what Kitty wants to ask. What if it's actually something about Alex?

"Are you…"

"Am I?" *Annie!* I think, but to be honest it makes me smile.

"You know…"

"No. What?" But Annie is smiling too now, and Kitty can hear it in her voice.

"Just tell me, you witch!"

They both burst out laughing and that moment is so full of relief, and release. It's magical; for me, at least.

"Yes. I am."

"You're...?" Now Kitty has to hear the words for herself.

"I'm pregnant." Annie finds herself gulp back a sob as she allows those words out. She isn't big on friendships and other than Alex and her siblings, she doesn't really have anyone she would confide in.

"Oh Annie," Kitty breathes. "Annie!" And she finds she's sobbing herself, at the thought of her sister's impending motherhood; at the fact that the air between them seems to be clear; at the idea of our family growing without me there to be a part of it. To help Annie learn to be a mum.

"I know. I can't believe it. It wasn't planned," she says matter-of-factly.

"But you're happy about it?"

"Yes. I – I think so." It's not like Annie to sound unsure about much in life – although I know she feels that way regularly – and it pulls at Kitty's heartstrings.

"You will be great, you know. You really will. We've had the best role model."

"Yes," Annie says quietly. "We have."

"She'd have been so happy," Kitty says.

"I hope so."

I am! I want to get inside their phone call, make them hear me. *I am so happy. You have no idea.*

"And what about Alex?" Again, Kitty feels she needs to ask about him. She will have to say his name, speak to him; see him. He's her brother-in-law, for god's sake. It's pointless pretending he doesn't exist.

142

Still, it feels uncomfortable, to be bringing him up again for the second time in this conversation.

"What about him?" Annie asks, fidgeting.

"He does know, doesn't he?" Kitty can hear something in Annie's voice. Even over the phone, she can read her.

"No, not yet." Annie speaks more confidently than she feels.

"Right…" Kitty wants to ask why not but is not sure it's her place to.

"I will tell him, of course."

"You'll have to at some point!" Kitty laughs.

"I know. I just… oh god, Kitty."

"What?"

"Well, at the moment, you're the only person other than my doctor who knows that I'm pregnant."

"Bloody hell, Annie. You haven't told Dad and Tom either?" Although, Kitty thinks, if she hasn't even told her own husband, it seems unlikely she'll have told their dad or brother.

"No. Only you."

"Oh Annie."

"I'm scared."

"You don't have to be, Annie. You will be brilliant, I am sure of it. And you have so many people around you. Supporting you. Loving you – and your baby."

Yes, thinks Annie, *but I think that there will be one fewer than you're assuming. I just don't know how to make that happen.*

Because the minute she tells Alex about the baby, she knows full well what his reaction will be. She can just picture his face, full of disbelief; his goofy grin plastered across it. And, while she's pissed off with him still, for what happened on New Year's Eve, she doesn't hate him. Far from it. That stupid situation has actually done her a favour, which makes her feel awful, but that's the fact of the matter. He deserves better than her, but she knows that she is going to have to break his heart.

15

Tom checks himself in the mirror for the umpteenth time. He looks very handsome but then I would think that, wouldn't I? I am, and always have been, every inch the proud mum.

He is my baby – which the girls always accused me of, and I always denied, but they were right really. Not that I loved them any less, and not that I tried to hold him back in any way; I loved seeing him develop and become independent, but it was always Tom I could rely on for a hug or even to just cast a thought my way, that perhaps I might not have had a good day. Or maybe that I might be tired, or needed a bit of time to relax. Not that he was perfect, he certainly had his moments, but I think perhaps as he was my last baby he always retained just a little piece of that status in my heart. I never had any other babies to replace him.

His thoughtfulness will, I hope, stand him in good stead with Cecily. Coupled with the influence of his sisters' double act when it comes to women's rights and general decency, I think he's a catch – as both his sisters had told him. But then I would, wouldn't I?

It's a thrill now, being with him as he readies himself. He's excited and nervous, in equal measures. *It's just a drink,* he tells himself.

Exactly. It's just a drink, Tom.

Interestingly, he turns as if he's heard me, but he shakes his head. Smiles a self-deprecating smile into the mirror, checks his phone for the time and to make sure she hasn't sent him any last-minute backing-out message. No, he's fine, but he'd better run. He doesn't want to be late.

It's been tricky, agreeing on the right place for this date. In our town, everyone knows him, but they don't know her. Cecily and her parents live about four miles away, close to another small market town, where of course everybody knows her. There is no way that she's going to have a date at the pub where she works – even though the Old Man and the Well is a great pub – and they've agreed to get the train to Shrewsbury, where there are so many more options, and less chance of being observed. They both feel more comfortable with that.

After a last-minute dash across the train tracks, with about one minute to spare before the barriers come down, Tom makes it onto the platform in time to see the train draw in. He spies her waving from a window. He smiles. Just her face reminds him he doesn't need to feel nervous; not really.

"Hi," he says as he sinks into the seat opposite her.

"Hello. You just made it, then?"

"Just!"

"Me too. I stopped in at the shop to get these…" She pulls two cans of ready-mixed rum and coke from her bag. "Fancy one?"

Tom grins. "That would be lovely."

She grins back, opens both the cans, and hands one over.

"Cheers," says Tom, raising his drink to her.

"Cheers," she echoes, and they both smile and then busy themselves with a sip of their drinks, feeling far too pleased with themselves and with each other, and suddenly very self-conscious.

We are pushing at the very edge of winter now and it feels more like spring so they decide to take a walk along the riverside and then find a pub in town where they can have a drink and maybe something to eat. The wide path is busy with walkers, dogs, joggers, families with little kids on balance bikes. It pushes Tom and Cecily closer together and he is tempted to take her hand but – *Not yet*, he thinks and a vision of his sisters in miniature, one on each of his shoulders, drifts into his head. *Don't be presumptuous*, Kitty warns him. *Let her make the first move*, advises Annie.

Imagining them like that makes him smile and then, remembering that they don't seem to be speaking to each other, he sighs.

Cecily looks at him. "Everything OK?"

"Oh, yeah. Yes." He pulls himself together, smiling. "Great, in fact."

"Good." She can see his smile is genuine but she knows there is something on his mind. She is good, this girl. *Young woman*, I correct myself, also channelling Kitty and Annie. She barely knows him, yet, but already she can read him.

"Tell me about your family," Tom says.

"My family?"

"Yes. You know all about mine, and you've already met them all! What's your family like? Are you... do you still have your parents? Brothers? Sisters?" As he asks this, Tom's chest tightens. Has he gone down a painful route? Thankfully, Cecily doesn't look disturbed by the questions.

"Yes, well you met my dad, at Christmas. At the long barrow."

"Of course." Tom casts his mind back to the impromptu carol concert, remembering a kind-faced, quiet man who had helped Cecily lock up for the night.

"And I'm very lucky to still have Mum, as well."

"You live with them?"

"Yes, at the moment."

"We always feel like we need to add 'at the moment', don't we? Our generation, I mean," Tom adds. "Like it's a matter of shame, or we've failed in some way."

"Yes! Exactly that," Cecily says. "But it's bloody expensive, renting."

"I just feel like we've missed the boat, somehow.

And it's not us that should be ashamed, it's the generations before us, who've bought up all the houses and pushed up the prices, and built themselves lovely little property empires."

"It's all those programmes as well, isn't it? *Homes Under the Hammer. Escape to the Country.*"

"*A Place in the Sun*," groans Tom. "'Oh, I've only got a budget of five million pounds, so I need you to help me find my dream holiday home where I can spend six months a year because I don't have to work anymore'."

Cecily laughs. "I'd just be happy with my own flat."

"Same." Tom thinks of Kitty in her place, where Olly used to live, and which she now has all to herself. He's not jealous as such, but envious. Though he couldn't leave Graham right now anyway.

"One day."

"Maybe."

They are walking so closely that their arms regularly brush each other's, and – privileged as I am – I know they are both feeling the same way. It's coming, I think. But I hope that they can enjoy this time right now. There is nothing like that magical feeling, when you're first with somebody you really, really like. And although it's filled with nerves and self-doubt, it's also thrilling, exciting, and brimming with promise.

"But back to your family," says Tom. "Do you have any brothers or sisters?"

"No," Cecily says. "Mum and Dad tried, I think, but

in the end they had to settle with just me."

"I'm sure they weren't just settling," Tom turns his head and smiles at her and Cecily returns his look shyly.

"I've got cousins," she volunteers, "just a couple of years older than me, and they live round here, actually, so I get to hang out with them sometimes. It's a bit like having sisters."

"That's good. It's not bad, having sisters. Most of the time."

"Did you ever want a brother?"

Tom considers this. "No, I don't think that ever crossed my mind. To be honest, I didn't always fit in very well with the blokes at school. I wasn't into football, or rugby, or cars. Too in touch with my feminine side," he grins.

"That's not a bad thing."

They both smile to themselves.

Dusk is closing in on the town as they pass the children's playground. Both glance at it, Tom remembering family trips when he and the girls were much younger. I loved those times, watching them zoom around the place, making easy, fleeting friendships with other children; smiling and laughing just for the joy of being alive, and the thrill of swinging higher and faster, or reaching the top of the climbing frame. Zipping down the biggest slide. Even now, with darkness fast approaching, there are a few stragglers squeezing the last drops of fun out of the day. Tom turns his head to look at them, and he pictures me sitting on the bench just over there, smiling at him. His happiness falters for a moment but he pushes on through. He thinks he is doing well; coping well; accepting of the fact I've died, but he doesn't see that what he's doing is a form of denial. I worry that it will have to catch up with him sometime. But perhaps, just perhaps, this thing with Cecily will help to carry him through.

They find a table at a riverside pub and sit opposite each other, which Tom immediately regrets. While it's lovely to be able to talk and to see her face, her smile, her thoughtful look, the physical proximity of the walk is now lost, and he longs to be able to feel her next to him again.

Still, this way they can talk, and they do, about everything. School, university, work, music, comedy, books, nature, climate change, music (again), the long barrow, religion, philosophy, politics... you can see the way the topics develop as the evening goes on, and the alcohol level rises.

"We should eat something!" Cecily says. "But it's so nice here."

They have a view of the river from their table, and the reflection of the streetlights twinkle prettily on the flowing water.

"We could just get some chips and garlic bread or something, if they're still doing food."

"That sounds great," says Cecily.

Tom stands and picks up their glasses.

"Same again as well?"

"Yes please."

When he returns, he's extremely pleased to see that Cecily has moved up to the next seat, leaving her chair free for him. "I thought it would be easier to share this way," she says.

"Good plan."

Neither of them are fooled by this transparent ploy and as Tom sits down, he pulls his chair slightly closer to hers.

"Sorry," Tom says, as his knee touches hers.

"I'll let you off," she smiles and turns to him and, with their faces just inches apart, Tom looks into Cecily's eyes and recognises something there.

Yes, I think. *Exactly.*

Haltingly, he moves his face forwards slightly and their lips meet, briefly.

"Is that alright?" he asks softly.

"Yes," she breathes, kicking herself for sounding like a love interest in a film, but then he is kissing her, and her head empties of any thought but of Tom. His closeness, his warmth, and how utterly delightful he is.

Now, I know I'm his mum, and I am a bit biased, but she is absolutely right.

16

Soon enough, it's Kitty's birthday weekend, and she finds herself both looking forward to and dreading coming back.

There is nothing like the comfort of returning home, if you are lucky enough to have a happy, loving place to return to. But for Kitty there is the prospect of my absence, which she is still not used to, and which she fears will hit her harder this time as it's been such a while since she's been back.

Then there is Alex.

Annie, she is not too worried about. Since that phone call, when they cleared the air, Kitty and Annie have been in touch more regularly. Mostly WhatsApps, but Kitty regularly checks in with her sister to make sure she's OK and to ask how she's feeling.

Not too bad, Annie says. **No morning sickness. Just a bit of a weird thing where everything smells a lot stronger. And I don't want to drink tea, either.**

That is weird.

I know.

And have you told Alex?

No. Not yet.

Shit, Kitty thinks, but she doesn't say so. In fact, she doesn't know what to say, but she can't leave Annie unanswered. However, Annie is already typing another message.

I will do. Soon. I'm just working it out.

Working what out? Kitty wants to ask, but she is loath to get too close with questions involving Alex. She is skating on thin ice there, she thinks. She still can't believe that Annie hasn't given her a harder time about the kiss, and feels bad that Alex may be taking the brunt of it all, when she was not entirely blameless.

Kitty remembers how she'd felt at Christmas when Alex was around, and that time at the long barrow on Christmas Day when he'd stood up for her, daring to cross Annie, and she'd felt... what? Something. Was it just gratitude, though? Tied up with the safe familiarity of somebody she has known for so long. Mixed with her aching heart from missing Olly, even though she kind of hates him.

OK. Well I guess you won't be able to hide it too much longer!

Although Annie, Kitty thinks, is probably one of those women on whom a pregnancy barely shows. While the two sisters look alike facially, Annie is more angular and straight-backed, in comparison to Kitty's slightly softer curves. Funny how their bodies kind of fit their personalities – not that what their bodies look like is anybody else's business, as they would rightly chastise me for this thought.

Kitty's message goes unanswered for some time. *Have I said something terribly wrong?* she worries. She is relieved to see Annie is typing again.

No, I know. And I can't go on not telling him. I think I'll wait till after the weekend. Then I'll tell him. This weekend's all about you anyway.

Kitty smiles at this.

Ah well it's not. It's about all of us. Back together again.

And Cecily.

And Cecily! Brilliant. Is Tom happy?

I don't think he's stopped smiling.

Ah that's lovely.

I know. And she is really nice. Good for him, I think.

Tom's big sisters both smile to themselves at the thought of him having maybe found love at last, and both try to push away their own increasingly cynical view of relationships, in the hope that maybe for Tom it will work out better.

"Kitty!" Graham hugs his daughter and fights the urge to never let her go. Often, he feels like he just wants somebody to hold him, support him, so that he can let go. Give in. But he knows he should not be looking to his children for this. Still, he appreciates the physical closeness of his younger daughter, and her very real solid – living – presence. Because now that I have gone, he is alert to the possibility that any one of them could die; of course, he has always known this is a possibility but never really believed it could happen. He didn't spend too much time worrying about that kind of thing. My illness, and my death, have brought it all into sharp focus. And if anything should happen to any of our three children, he doesn't know what he would do.

But right now, it's Kitty's birthday, and she's come home, and he hasn't seen her for so long, and it's her first birthday without her mum, and he needs to look after her. He needs to make sure it's a good day for her.

"I made you a cake!" he says, even though he'd meant to keep it as a surprise.

"Dad!" she laughs. "That's so nice!"

She follows him into the house, where Cecily and Tom are in the kitchen. Their pink cheeks don't go unnoticed by Kitty, who is sure that they have hurriedly extricated themselves from each other at the sound of her entrance.

"Hello sis!" Tom says, stepping forward and hugging her.

"Hello," she smiles into his shoulder, feeling wrong-footed as his older sister that she should be shorter than him. "It's so good to see you. And hi Cecily," she pulls away and smiles at Tom's girlfriend. "How are you?"

"I'm good thanks," Cecily smiles a little shyly.

"I've got Cecily to thank for your cake actually," Graham admits. "I forgot to put the baking powder in the first one. It's out there on the bird table. Cecily's talked me through my second attempt."

"That sounds like a good thing," Kitty smiles. "Let's see it then!"

"No, no, not till we're singing Happy Birthday!"

"I knew you couldn't keep it a surprise, Dad," Tom chides. "Fancy a coffee, Kitty?"

"Yes please. Annie and Alex not here yet?" she asks, hoping she sounds suitably nonchalant.

"No, they're coming later. I think they're shopping or something this morning."

"Oh, OK." A few hours' respite then, before she has to face them both in person. Kitty has been preparing herself for this, and coaching herself. *It's just Annie, and Alex*, she keeps telling herself. Only she can't forget the last times she saw them both in person.

Mavis, who is older and a little more deaf than she was, takes a couple of minutes to work out Kitty is home but when she does she comes bounding through like a puppy, throwing herself at Kitty and crying and whimpering.

"Alright, alright," Kitty laughs. "I've missed you too!"

"Come on, let's go and sit down," Tom says, piling a tray with cups and a jug of milk, and a full cafetière. They go through to the lounge, where Graham takes the fireside chair, Tom and Cecily the settee, and Kitty the other armchair, where she is immediately pinned down by Mavis licking her face.

Tom sets out the cups and pours in the milk, then Cecily picks up the cafetière.

"Shall I be mother?" she says, then she checks herself, her cheeks reddening. "I'm sorry. What a stupid thing to say."

"No it wasn't!" Kitty protests, pushing Mavis gently away. "Don't be daft, it's just a saying."

Cecily and Tom both look gratefully at her, while Graham apparently hasn't noticed anyway. He's away with the fairies momentarily, and his focus only returns to the room when Tom hands him his cup of coffee.

"Thanks, son," he smiles, and he looks at Kitty. "So, what's new in your life?"

She tells them about the kennels, and Meg, and how the slightly warmer weather means life is a bit easier, but how they need to do some fundraising to keep the rescue kennels going. There are puppies, from the pregnant bitch that came to them in January, but these are all off to their new homes in the coming weeks.

"It must be tough," says Cecily, sympathetically.

"It can be. It's really hard for Meg, particularly. She goes without a lot so that dogs don't have to. Not like you, spoiled mutt." Kitty rubs Mavis's ears.

"You should do a dog show or something," Tom suggests.

"That's not a bad idea, little brother. I'll mention that to Meg."

Just as Kitty and Tom are grinning at each other, they hear the back door and their older sister calling, "Hello?"

Tom tries to read Kitty's expression but she's playing it cool. Besides, now that she is in the situation, she just needs to press on with it. The anticipation has been almost the worst thing. Nevertheless, she can feel her heartbeat quicken slightly.

She stands and Mavis, who has just settled into her lap for a kip, grumbles as she lands on the floor. "I'd better go and say hello," says Kitty.

She walks through the hallway. "Hi," she calls back, hoping she sounds normal. Graham, she thinks, won't notice either way at the moment, but Tom would almost certainly pick up on something. She finds her sister taking off her boots in the hallway.

"Hi," Annie says. She straightens up and Kitty can't help a quick glance at her sister's tummy to see if the pregnancy is visible but no, she doesn't think you'd know anything to look at Annie.

Kitty steps forward and hugs her sister. Annie is stiff for a moment but then relaxes, and reciprocates. Kitty finds her eyes fill with tears. She keeps her head on Annie's shoulder for a moment.

"It's OK," Annie says.

Kitty looks at her. "Really?"

"Really."

She seems older. There is a more grown-up air about her. It's to do with the baby, Kitty supposes. Annie has crossed, or is crossing, a bridge that she has yet to come to herself – assuming she will ever get to it. She looks past Annie's shoulder, towards the door.

"He's not coming," Annie says.

"What?"

"Alex. He's not coming."

"Oh. Erm."

"I told him not to. I think it's for the best." Annie's mouth is a straight line, and this Kitty recognises. Her mind is made up and there will be no changing it.

160

"OK…"

"I told him about the baby, too. I told him last night. I realised I couldn't wait any longer."

"Oh, good. That's a relief, at least." It is also a relief that he isn't coming, Kitty thinks, although she'll have to face him sometime.

"Yes, it is… in a way. But I also told him I don't want to be married to him anymore."

17

Friday night and Alex was late back, whereas Annie had made sure she shut down her computer as soon as she could, and left the office promptly at ten past five.

"Goodnight, Sam," she said to the security guard. "Have a good weekend." Then she kicked herself, thinking he was probably working all weekend.

"You too." He'd just smiled and Annie, unusually empathetic, had considered what it might be like to work on the security desk in an office where people came and went with their expensive clothes and their sizeable egos. Did Sam resent them? She hoped not, but she thought that if the boot was on the other foot, she might feel some level of bitterness. Probably Sam was just a better person than her.

No, Annie, I wanted to tell her. *You're not a bad person. Far from it.*

But knowing what the evening ahead meant, Annie felt like the worst person in the world.

She'd had every intention of waiting a little longer but the onset of sleepless, anxious nights changed her mind. It couldn't be good for her, or the baby. It had been very difficult to decide what to do, and how to play it. She could make Alex's favourite dinner, but would that just set him up to fall even further? He might see what she was doing and consider that she had a 'date night' planned (even with her burden of guilt, that phrase still made her shudder). Instead, she had opted for a good bottle of wine – mostly for him, though she thought that just maybe she'd have a small glass as well. Dutch courage.

Picking up a bottle at the small Tesco, she walked down the hill to the train station and as she did so she realised that her spare hand was gently resting on her stomach. The unconscious act made her smile, despite everything, but as soon as she was on the train, she began to feel the distinct discomfort and nerves of a guilty conscience.

He's the one who should feel guilty, she tried to tell herself, but she was convincing nobody. Even though he had kissed Kitty – her own sister – on New Year's Eve, if she was very honest that paled in comparison to her treatment of him over the years, and to what she was about to put him through.

Impending motherhood seems to have brought out this new side to Annie, which consists of... well, feelings. Not only that, but she has a renewed sense of purpose. She is ambitious, career-wise, and she always has been, but now she has something outside of work that is going to require just as much

163

determination. She has thought and thought about Alex, and whether she and he could make things work together, but she always comes up with the same answer – and the same feeling of fatigue at the thought of spending the rest of her life with him. She can already see what he'll be like as a dad, and she knows he will be lovely, but she also knows that he will drive her up the wall.

She reads, illicitly, forums of new mums, who find their husbands disappointing; frustrating; infuriating. And these were women who had wanted their husbands to be involved; partners in this parenting lark. Annie, typically contrary, has found that she does not want a partner in this. She thinks that in contrast to these other men, Alex might actually play his part: get involved; try his hand at bottle-feeding and getting up in the night. Read parenting manuals and have opinions on weaning, and vaccinations, and 'tummy time', and god knows what else. Why, then, when all these other women bemoan the fact that their husbands seem so disconnected from it all, does Annie fear the opposite from Alex? *What's actually wrong with me?* she berates herself.

Nothing, Annie. Nothing is wrong with you. You are just with the wrong person. I know that better now than ever.

When she arrived home, the house was empty, and in darkness, the curtains still drawn, even though she'd asked Alex to open them before he left for work. Annie hates to be in darkness when there is natural light to make the most of. I was just the same.

Going from room to room in a huff, Annie drew the curtains and blinds, even though she knew there was only an hour or so of daylight left. It was the principle of the matter, she thought haughtily, then a blanket of guilt fell over her again.

As it was, Alex did not get home until about eight, having called at the gym on the way home. He was starting to feel the benefit of it, he thought, running his right hand lightly over his left biceps. He liked the feeling.

"Hello?" he called tentatively, noting that all the curtains were shut and remembering he had forgotten to open them before he left that morning. Damn, Annie would be annoyed at him. Little did he know she'd actually been round the house opening them and then once more, closing them as darkness moved in.

"In here," Annie called, and he'd gone into their smart, professionally-decorated lounge, where Annie was sitting with the fire crackling merrily (the traitor), and a bottle of red wine breathing on the hearth.

"Hi," he bent and tentatively kissed her.

She managed a thin smile. "Good day?"

"Yeah, not bad thanks. Better now I've hit the gym."

Hit the gym. It was just the kind of expression that Annie hated, and it jarred for a moment and then she found a sadness seeping in, that she could be so harsh to this man in front of her, over something so trivial. After all, what did it matter, what expression he might choose to use? Despite everything, Annie knew Alex to be a kind, pleasant person, and she knew she couldn't toy with him, with this bottle of wine and warming fire suggesting a lovely cosy evening ahead.

"I think we should split up," she said. Just like that. Before she had the chance to think again. She watched his face fall. His eyes met hers, then looked away while he considered what she'd just said. Had he heard it correctly? His face was an open book, to Annie, and she felt like she could read his very thoughts, as he tried to make sense of this sudden bombshell.

"You think we should…?"

"Split up," she confirmed.

"But… but… Annie, no."

"I do, Alex. I'm sorry. I do."

"Because of Kitty?"

"No, Alex. That has nothing to do with it." Although it had, in a way. It had kickstarted this process, made her realise she did not actually feel the way she probably should about it; about him.

He sat down, shattered.

Annie poured him a glass of wine. "I really am sorry, Alex."

"We can talk it through," he countered. "I can do better. Be better."

The words were like a blow to her stomach.

"It's not you," she said, aware that she was dangerously close to the 'it's not you, it's me' line. "It's not to do with Kitty, and it's not to do with you not doing well enough. You are a good person; a lovely person, and you always have been. I just – it's just – this doesn't feel right to me anymore." She stopped just short of saying 'and I don't know if it ever did'. "We were young when we got together and you know I hadn't had many relationships before."

"Me neither," Alex said heartbreakingly eagerly. "We learned together."

"We did," Annie said. "And I am grateful for that, and for you. But I've not been able to stop thinking about the future lately, Alex, and I'm so sorry but I just can't see us having one together. Not happily. And I do, honestly, think that we both deserve to be happy."

"I can make you happy."

"I wish you could, Alex. And I wish I could make you happy."

"You do," he protested, tears squeezing from his eyes.

"Do I, though? Really? If you're very honest. I am nitpicky, and a nag, and I'm just not very nice to you, Alex. I've thought for a long time that it's because I'm not a very nice person and there is still a part of me that thinks that's true – but at the same time I think it might just be that we're not right for each other. Anymore." There was no point in letting him think she believed they'd never been right for each other.

Alex put his glass down, untouched. To his credit, alcohol was the last thing he wanted in that moment.

"I can't believe it," he said, and it was those four words that finally brought forth Annie's tears.

"Me neither." She was out of her chair and hugging him. She wanted to take it back, to make it right, to plug his hurt. But no, she thought, this was the first step taken. And it was the right path she was on. But it didn't make it any easier. She took a deep breath. Sat back. Made him look at her. "Alex."

"Yes?"

"There's something else."

"You've met somebody, haven't you? I knew it. And I deserve it, after what I did…"

"No, no, it's not that." A fleeting sense of irritation, that he saw things in such simple terms as to think that must be the only explanation. "Alex, I'm pregnant."

That was the hardest part, even for me as a spectator. I felt like I was holding my breath, and I watched as Alex once again struggled to comprehend what his wife (for the time being, at least) was saying.

"You're…?"

"Pregnant," she confirmed.

"Is it… mine?"

"Yes!" she exploded finally. "Of course it's yours, Alex. God, I haven't been with anyone else. I wouldn't do that. I couldn't."

"But then, how can we split up?"

"Because we have to," Annie said. "We have to."

"Can't we just talk it through, work on it? Go to couples' therapy?"

"Alex," Annie's voice was softer again. "If I thought it would help, I would do that. But I don't. I can't. My mind's made up. Honestly, I've been through it so many times, and I always come back to the same answer."

"But we're having a baby," he said plaintively.

"I know, I know, and it will still be us. It will still be *our* baby."

"Well of course it bloody will." At last, a flash of anger across his features. "You're not taking that away from me as well."

"No, Alex. I'm not. I wouldn't dream of it. I wouldn't want to."

"Good." He took a gulp of his wine, then another.

Now what? wondered Annie. She had said what she wanted to say, but now what? It was Friday night, and not even nine o'clock. She'd just told her husband that she was pregnant and that she wanted to split up with him. They couldn't very well turn on the TV and watch what remained of *Would I Lie to You?*

Thankfully, Alex had an answer. "I'll go to Mum and Dad's. They're away this weekend. I think I need to go and sort my head out. And maybe some space will help you sort out yours."

"Some space would be good," Annie acknowledged. "But Alex, I won't be changing my mind. You do need to know that."

"I know," he said, and he stood and left the room. She heard him go upstairs, and some banging of drawers and doors – presumably Alex getting some things together – then she heard him come down the stairs and head towards the door. A jingle of car keys as he picked them off the hook. She followed him outside, where the rain was battering the garden, bouncing off the windowsills and the car roof.

"Alex…" She had to half-shout to be heard.

He turned, his face illuminated by the light from the kitchen window. His hair already soaked and plastered to his head. She had never seen him look so miserable. "I can't, Annie. I can't say anything. I need to go."

"Okay." She watched him get in the car, and drive away, and for a moment she panicked. Had she done the right thing? She had changed the course of her life forever. But as the sound of his car vanished into the distance, she took a deep breath, turned her face up into the rain, feeling its vitality. She put a hand on her stomach. Took another deep breath. She'd done it.

Annie went back into the house and stripped off her wet clothes, grabbing some pyjamas from the basket of washing that was waiting to be ironed.

In the lounge, she put another log on the fire, and the cork in the bottle of wine. Seeing Alex's half-drunk glass on the table, she picked it up and took it into the kitchen, washing the remains of his wine down the sink. She felt relieved, and fidgety, all at once. She wanted to celebrate. She wanted to cry. She wanted to shout.

What a night, she thought. *What a night.* And suddenly, she was heaving with sobs, and gasping.

"Mum!" she cried out, "Mum! What have I done?"

And it was awful, not being able to comfort her, or tell her how brave she was, and that what she had done was exactly what she was meant to do.

18

I am just so grateful that my family are together today – for Kitty's birthday, and for Annie's sake too. Even so, it feels different; and I don't just mean because I am not there. Was it always like this? It seemed to me that our family life was pretty steady. I don't want to say dull, but at least predictable. There was me and Graham (let's put Nick aside for the moment), Annie and Alex, Kitty and Olly (though I had hoped she'd see sense with him eventually), Tom and, of course, Mavis.

Even before the incomers (Alex and Olly), there was stability. We all knew our places. The girls were a duo, and it was Tom who was sometimes a little on the side-lines, unless the girls had fallen out with each other. Another reason, I suppose, that I may have given Tom more of my attention, but now it seems the tables have turned.

They go to the Old Man and the Well for lunch, Cecily having assured them that it wouldn't be at all awkward, whilst secretly wishing they'd chosen another place. It is a little bit strange, being waited on by her colleagues, but as a newcomer to the family (still auditioning, in fact), she feels very strongly that it is her place to go along with whatever they want to do. Besides, she is also very aware that this is the first of the family birthdays without me there. She will do whatever is necessary to make it as easy as possible for Tom and his family.

It's raining hard as they arrive at the pub and they dash through the car park, coats pulled over their heads, laughing and exclaiming at the terrible weather. When they step inside, they are greeted by the warmth of the fire and a laugh from one of the regulars.

"Lovely day," he says.

"It is that," agrees Graham, peeling off his raincoat.

"Here, hang them up there near the radiator," the landlady advises them.

"Thanks, Marianne," says Cecily.

"No problem. Now, this must be Tom, I presume?"

"Erm, yes." Cecily flushes slightly.

"Pleased to meet you," Marianne shakes Tom's hand. "You've got a good one here, you know."

Cecily's face turns an even brighter red.

"I know," Tom just smiles. "Thank you."

Kitty, seeing Cecily's embarrassment, ushers her over to the rectangular table which has a reserved sign on it. They take their seats, Graham at one end, Tom and Cecily on his left-hand side, Kitty and Annie on his right. Annie has been very vague about Alex's absence, but Tom is aware that she and Kitty have been whispering together. He wants to know what's going on but doesn't feel like he can ask. It's frustrating for him; these last few weeks he's been the only person Kitty's really spoken to, and he and Annie have spent more time together, without Kitty, than they ever have before. Now it seems it's back to normal, with his sisters thick as thieves and him feeling like the little brother once more.

The difference now, thinks Tom, is that he's the one with a partner. The only one, he thinks guiltily of Graham, sitting alone at the head of the table. Tom casts a sidelong glance at Cecily. Can he call her his partner? It's early days still and perhaps that's stretching things a bit. Still, she's come to a family celebration, which shows some level of willingness and commitment. Or so he hopes, at least.

Kitty is great at making conversation with Cecily, and Tom begins to feel more settled again – and grateful for his sister's easy, thoughtful manner. At one point, Kitty sends a smile sailing Tom's way, which eases his feeling of antipathy even further.

Kitty is so glad to be back with her family, and relieved that she and Annie are OK. More than OK, in fact. Annie has taken her into her confidence and, even though their two-year age gap is irrelevant now that they are both adults, Kitty still looks up to her big sister, just as Tom feels like the perennial little brother. Annie is the one Kitty wanted to be like, as soon as she was really aware of her. As she grew from baby to toddler to schoolchild. She saw her sister riding a bike, and she wanted to do it. Roller skating, reading, playing netball, learning the piano (not all at the same time) – Kitty saw Annie develop these skills and she wanted to do the same. Sensible, clever Annie was always a step ahead and always seemed so much more grown-up. So now, even knowing Annie's troubles and difficulties and struggles to fit in, Kitty still feels honoured that her older sister values and trusts her.

When she smiles at Tom, it's pure love for him. She's so pleased he's met Cecily, and she's never seen him so into somebody before. It's a relief as well that he seems to have made a more sensible choice than either she or Annie did. Cecily is lovely, as she already knew. *This one has legs*, she thinks, and she stifles a laugh at the odd phrase, which has popped into her head from who knows where.

"You look happy, Kitty," Graham says.

"I am thank you, Dad. It's being back with all of you. Though I wish…"

"I know." He puts his hand on hers. "We'll always wish that." His eyes gleam with tears.

Cecily, seeing, wishes there was something she could do. She'd like to raise a toast to me, she thinks, but feels it would be far too presumptuous. It's funny; in another situation, at the long barrow, she would be the one guiding them. She might very well propose a toast. She'd certainly mention me by name. Now, she is a guest at their table, and she needs to behave accordingly. So she returns her eyes to the dessert menu, although of course she knows it off by heart.

One thing she has been able to do, having the advantage of working here, is arrange for Kitty's birthday cake to be stored in the kitchen, ready to be brought out – right about now, in fact. Graham and Tom are aware of this, but they hadn't had the chance to mention it to Annie, who looks almost as surprised as Kitty when Marianne, the landlady, begins the walk across the pub carrying a chocolate cake aglow with thirty-two candles.

"No way!" Kitty exclaims. "You never made that, Dad?"

"Well, like I say, with a little help from Cecily."

"More like a lot of help!" Tom says proudly.

"Thank you, Cecily!" Kitty beams at her.

"My pleasure," says Cecily, smiling. She remembers me saying to her about the cakes – how I'd always bake one for each of the children, no matter how old they were. And how it had been so bittersweet last year, baking each one and knowing that it would almost certainly be the last time. It was always chocolate for Kitty, lemon drizzle for Tom, and Victoria sponge for Annie – that was Graham's favourite, too. By the time his last birthday came around, I was too ill to make a cake, and it wasn't exactly the first thing on either of our minds anyway. So the last one I'd made him, I'd been in the kitchen with the door to the garden wide open, Mavis lying in the shade and the birds singing merrily away. I had hummed to myself as I'd broken the eggs, completely oblivious that this would be the final time I made a birthday cake for my husband.

When Cecily found Graham cursing in the kitchen earlier, she'd asked if she could help.

"I'm beyond help," he'd groaned, and she'd laughed.

"What's happened?"

"I've made this cake for Kitty but it's more like a bloody biscuit."

"I see what you mean. Did you put baking powder in the mix?"

"No, was I meant to?"

"It can help. Look, have you got enough ingredients to start again?"

"I don't know." Graham was close to tearing his hair out, his head in his hands on the counter. "I just wanted to make Kitty a cake like her mum used to."

"That's so nice," Cecily said, "she'll love it. And who doesn't enjoy a nice biscuit?"

Graham had looked up and she was pleased to see he was smiling.

"Come on," Cecily said. "Let's start again. I can help. Do you think a chocolate cake might be nice?" she suggested as though just plucking the idea out of the air.

"Do you know what? Yes, that's a good idea. Kitty likes a chocolate cake."

"Then this could all work out perfectly," Cecily had smiled. "Is this Ruth's recipe book?"

"Yes," Graham had looked mournfully at the book I'd kept, full of my notes and scribbled measurements.

"Great." Cecily, while always sympathetic, was keen to keep the momentum up, and Graham's mood, too. "Can you find the chocolate cake recipe, and we can make sure we've got everything we need?"

Graham had felt an overwhelming relief at somebody else taking this responsibility off his shoulders. He flicked through the pages, trying his best not to see the sadness in them, and he found what they needed. "Kitty will love this," he said, trying his best to be upbeat, and finding it was possible, with somebody there to help him.

And he was right. Kitty is deeply touched, and makes a mental note that they will have to do the same for her brother and sister, and indeed her dad. "Help me blow the candles out!" she implores now and all three of my children, and Cecily, lean towards the cake, laughing as they blow across at each other.

Graham picks up his phone and takes a picture. It's the first time he's felt compelled to take a photo since I died. It's good. I stand behind him, resting lightly on his shoulders while they all sing Happy Birthday.

Some of the other customers join in the singing and for a few brief moments I am secure in the knowledge that all of my family are smiling and happy. Uplifted.

Annie has driven, giving herself the perfect excuse not to partake in the prosecco Graham has ordered, and as she takes her merry carload back home, she falls into silence, contemplating how the lunch out provided a little respite from the reality of life, but now she was heading straight back into it.

Graham, in the passenger seat, looks across at her. "Everything alright, love?"

"What? Oh, yeah, fine thanks. Just thinking about work."

"Anything I can help with?"

"Oh no, thanks Dad, more of a human resources thing, really."

"Ah yes, work would be a lot easier without other people sometimes, wouldn't it?"

"And life in general!" she laughs. "I don't mean you, of course, or any of the rabble in the back."

"What about Alex?" he asks, gently.

She shoots a look at him. So he has noticed, I think. I wasn't sure. His thoughts on the matter have seemed incomplete, half-formed, like they pass through his head, the idea that something is wrong, but he just can't quite pull the different strands together.

"Hmm." Annie says.

"Are you having problems?"

"Sort of. Well, yes. Well." They are nearly home. Annie isn't sure what to say, but she knows she should really say something. As she pulls into the drive and turns off the engine she says, "Listen, I don't want to create a drama or anything, but I've got some news I need to share with you all."

Tom looks at Kitty, who doesn't meet his eye. She already knows what Annie's about to say, he can see that. It annoys him a bit. "What is it, Annie?" he asks. Cecily takes his hand. He squeezes it, grateful for her presence.

Annie is already regretting not waiting until they were at least out of the car first. She watches the windscreen wipers in their futile work, squeaking as they move to and fro. Raindrops pelt the car roof, banging on it like tiny little fists.

"You might as well know," she says, looking at Graham, gauging his reaction, "Alex and I are splitting up."

There is a silence, as Graham and Tom take this in. Cecily tries not to squirm, feeling very much out of place and wishing she could just open the car door and fall silently out so that the family could process this news together.

"And that's not all," Annie says. "I'm pregnant."

"Woah!" Tom gasps.

Kitty reaches a hand forward and squeezes their sister's shoulder. It wasn't how she would have chosen to break the news but she knows these things are not exactly Annie's forte.

Tom sees the gesture and he wants to beat that closeness. After all, he's been the one here for Annie lately. She and Kitty have barely spoken. Why is that, anyway? Has it got anything to do with this bombshell – these bombshells?

"Bloody hell, Annie, give it to us gently, why don't you?" Graham says, and his words break the hard silence. Everybody laughs in relief; even Annie.

"Sorry!" she says. "I just couldn't go any longer without saying anything. I couldn't do it at lunch because I didn't want to take the limelight from Kitty. It's her birthday, after all."

"I wouldn't have minded," Kitty says.

Sure, thinks Tom, although he's annoyed at himself for feeling so petty.

"Come on," Graham says, and I'm delighted to see him taking the lead. "Let's get in the house and put the kettle on. I'm gasping for a cuppa."

"I've gone off tea," Annie blurts out, keen now to share the strangeness of being pregnant. And doubly keen to keep the focus on that and not her failed marriage.

"I'll make you a hot chocolate," says Graham. He and his daughters go into the kitchen, while Tom and Cecily head off to the lounge.

"Well, I can't pretend I'm not shocked," Graham says.

"Sorry, Dad."

"Don't be sorry. I – well, I feel sorry for Alex, assuming this is your decision?"

"It is," she confirms.

"But I never thought you were exactly a perfect match."

"Really, Dad? I never noticed," Annie says sarcastically.

"Was I that obvious?" Graham looks crestfallen.

"You were great, Dad. I just knew that you weren't exactly Alex's biggest fan."

"Oh."

Kitty wants to stick up for Alex, but knows she'd be skating on very thin ice if she did. She stays quiet.

"But a baby," Graham says. "On your own? It's very hard work, you know."

"I know that, Dad. I'm scared," Annie says, tears spilling from her eyes. He steps forward and hugs her. Kitty takes her leave.

"Hi you two," she says as she steps through the lounge doorway, just in case she's interrupting anything.

"Hi," says Tom. "You knew about that, of course?" he asks before she's even sat down.

"Erm, yes, but only just."

"Really?"

"Yes, Annie told me this morning."

"Oh," Tom feels slightly better. He hasn't been as left out of things as he'd thought.

"About Alex, I mean. She did tell me about being pregnant. When you came to visit. Well, she thought she might be."

"Oh," Tom says again. That's a blow. "Is that why you two haven't been talking?" he asks bluntly, not able to understand why that would be the case.

Kitty glances at Cecily, who has her eyes on her phone, pretending to be engrossed in a message. "We haven't not been talking," Kitty says.

"Come on," says Tom. "You haven't been back here since Christmas and I've barely heard from you but Annie's said she hasn't spoken to you at all."

"Right. Well, I've just…"

"Don't say you've been focusing on your art! You'd still have had time for the odd call every couple of days."

"I've just needed some space."

Tom, seemingly from out of nowhere, feels a rush of emotions sweep through him. "Because of Mum?" he exclaims. "You're not the only one missing her, you know. We're all grieving. We're all heartbroken, but doesn't that mean we all need each other more than ever at the moment? And I've been here with, with Dad, who's here in physical form but away with the fairies half the time – and Annie, who is, well, Annie. I've needed you, Kitty, and you haven't been here."

Shut up, Tom, he is thinking, but he can't help himself.

"I'm sorry Tom," Kitty is crying now.

Cecily sits awkwardly, again wishing she could magic herself away. She should not have been here with them for the first of their birthdays without me. It seems obvious now. But she can't go back.

"No, I'm sorry," Tom says, looking at Cecily and squeezing her hand, then turning to Kitty. "I am, I'm not being fair, and it's your birthday, and I'm sorry, but I don't understand why you just removed yourself from our lives like you have."

"I haven't removed myself. I just…"

"Yeah, yeah, needed some space. But I don't get it. If you knew that Annie was pregnant, didn't you think that you might be needed more than ever? And what the hell's happened with her and Alex, anyway?" This last question bursts out of him as the full implication of their older sister's revelations hits him.

He feels a hand on his arm. "Tom," Cecily says gently. He turns to her, sees her kind eyes on his. "Maybe just leave it," she suggests.

"You're right. Sorry," he says to Cecily more than Kitty.

"I think I'd better go though," she says.

"No, don't. Don't. I'm sorry." He lifts her hand and kisses it.

"No, I'd better. I'll call you later."

Seeing the sense in her going, and not blaming her for wanting to make an escape, Tom stands with Cecily. "I'll see you out."

"Tom," Kitty says. "I'll tell you. I'll explain, OK?"

"OK."

Tom walks Cecily to the train station and they stand hugging each other on the platform, grateful that the rain has at least stopped for now.

"It was always going to be a hard day," Cecily says.

"For all of you. All these firsts, they're unbearable."

Tom shivers. The wind blows cold along the railway tracks but it's more than that. The world seems to have become so jumbled up, and very little makes sense these days. He holds Cecily tighter.

She kisses him on the cheek as the train approaches. "Don't be angry at Kitty," she says. "Or Alex."

"I won't be," Tom says. "Thank you, Cecily. Thanks for coming today, and I'm sorry it all got a bit dramatic."

"Don't apologise," she says. "I'm honoured to have been invited. Your family are great."

He smiles then and waits until the train has moved off before heading home. It's only as he is walking back along the high street, dodging the puddles that have pooled on the pavement and at the kerbsides, that Cecily's words come back to him. What did she mean, about not being angry with Alex?

19

"Fancy a walk?" Tom asks Kitty shortly after he gets back from the station.

"Sure!" she smiles, eager to put things on a better footing. "I could do with clearing my head, I'm not used to wine at lunchtime."

"Great. I'll get Mavis ready."

"Should we ask Dad, and Annie?"

"I think they're both having a rest," Tom says. He knows full well they are; he suggested it to them both. Cecily's words have been playing on his mind and he's determined to find out what's been going on. And how Cecily is involved in all of this.

They set off companionably, pleased that – could it possibly be? – a little bit of sunshine is bouncing off the puddles which line the roads and fill the potholes.

"Let's go down to the woods," says Kitty. "I haven't been there in years."

"It's Saturday," says Tom, "all the kids'll be there vaping and getting up to no good!" He grins at Kitty. There was certainly a time when both of them would have been getting up to no good in the woods as well.

"Is the old shelter there?" Kitty asks.

"Yes, well it's more like a new shelter now."

"Ooh, fancy!"

"I definitely wouldn't call it fancy. I'll let you see for yourself."

They turn off the main road and head down the path, opting for the right fork which takes them alongside the smaller of two rivers. In truth, 'river' seems a grand word for these small waterways, although after the weeks of recent rain, they are punching above their weight, the murky brown waters high up and moving at quite a rate.

Mavis scampers up and down, wondering whether to go in, but a quick, sharp word from Tom is enough to make her mind up. She'll stick to the muddy path, thanks very much.

After a short walk, they reach the little bridge. "The water's nearly over the top of it!" says Kitty.

"Yeah, it's been like this a lot lately," Tom says, and looks along to the tall trees a couple of hundred yards away. "And look, there's the egret."

"The what?"

"Egret. Well, a little egret, to be exact. I spotted him a couple of weeks back. He's like a small heron."

"Are you sure he's a he, Tom?"

"No, Kitty, I'm not, but it's a fifty-fifty chance, isn't it?"

"Alright!" she smiles, slightly taken aback at the way he's snapped, but as usual not willing to react unduly. She turns her head. "Oh my! I see what you mean about the shelter!"

There is a spot just past the little bridge where for decades the local kids have come to hang out after school, at weekends, during the holidays. They've banked up the earth so that there are a few jumps for those who like to come by bike, and there used to be a semi-shelter fashioned from branches and camouflage netting. The kids made it themselves and, unbeknown to the children, some of the local adults came along and made it safe one day. Yes, those kids might be having an illicit cigarette or a few ciders, but they weren't causing trouble, and it was nothing more than many of us had got up to in our day. We just wanted to make the place safe – and as watertight as possible – appreciating that there is not a great deal for youngsters to do in this small town.

Now, though, the old shelter is all but gone. It was ripped down by a few older teens, who actually were out to cause trouble (and succeeded, eventually, in creating more trouble for themselves than anybody else) and has been replaced over time by a huge bright blue tarp, strung up with orange nylon rope, and furnished with some rusty old chairs, the origin of which I have no idea. There is a firepit, and bags of rubbish. A big old stick is suspended from one of the larger trees over the water, but I hope that is not in use till the weather has warmed up and the engorged river waters are much reduced.

It's a bit of an eyesore these days, to be honest, but it's still a place for kids to come and, by and large, the children these days are no more trouble than in years past, no matter what some of the local Facebook-page brigade might have you believe.

"Takes me back, though!" Kitty says. "We had some laughs here, didn't we?"

"Yeah." Tom thinks of how Kitty and her friends let him and some of his mates join them, when they were really quite young. His eyes meet hers and he gives her a grin. "Guess what I've got?"

"What?"

He pulls a slim joint from his pocket.

"No! Tom! Where did you get that from?"

"I've usually got a bit on me," he says airily. "I mean, I don't smoke like I used to, but I do enjoy a little one when I'm walking Mavis sometimes."

"You dark horse! I haven't smoked for years. I assumed you'd stopped, too."

"Hey, I'm a musician. And you're an artist. This is practically compulsory."

"I don't know about that," Kitty says, watching her brother light up. He takes a couple of slow, deep drags and offers it to her. "Go on then," she says, suddenly swept up in a wish to be young and carefree once again. "Bloody hell!" She coughs, but takes another drag.

A few fat raindrops begin to push themselves through the branches, past the buds which will soon flourish and bring these woods to life once more.

"Shall we sit in there?" Tom gestures towards the shelter.

"Oh, I don't know. I think we're too old." Kitty hands the joint back to Tom.

"Come on!" he says. "At least we'll be dry."

"What if the kids come and beat us up, though?" asks Kitty, hot on Tom's heel. They both start laughing.

"These chairs are minging," Tom says.

"I know. I think I'd rather sit on the floor."

"We'll just stop for as long as it takes to smoke this," Tom says. "Then we'll move on."

Mavis is happy to hurtle around the nearby shrubbery, barking at squirrels and startling blackbirds. Tom and Kitty are quiet for a while.

"It's weird, isn't it?" says Tom.

"What, being here?"

"Well, yes, this – but everything. Mum. Dad. Annie. Alex."

He watches his sister's face but sees no discernible reaction. He hands her the joint. She waves it away.

"Yep. It is weird. All of it. And you and I are going to have a niece or nephew. Yet here we are sitting in the woods smoking weed!"

Tom's begun his course of conversation, though, and is unwilling to be distracted. He tries another tack.

"Is everything OK now, with you and Annie?"

"What? Oh, yeah," Kitty screws up her face in a 'it was something and nothing' kind of a way.

"What happened, Kitty?"

She looks at him.

"Really. What happened? I know something did." The smoke has gone to his head, and he feels pleasantly fuzzy, but he knows he must keep focused.

She gestures for him to hand the joint back to her. Takes a drag, feeling the smoke reach the back of her throat, then watches it emerge into the world as she exhales slowly. Should she tell him? It suddenly seems too hard not to.

"It sounds like more than it was," she warns him.

"OK…"

"But, well, Alex and I — "

"What?" He can't help reacting to the words 'Alex and I'.

"Hang on," she says. "Well, we kind of. Kissed."

"What?" Said again, with more fervour.

"Don't, Tom, OK? It was awful. Not the kiss. I mean, it was barely a kiss to be honest, but it should never have happened. Never."

"So why did it?" Tom is very black-and-white about these things, as I was at his age.

"I don't know," she moans, handing the joint back to him, though there is little left now. "I really don't know. It was New Year's Eve — "

"It happened at home?" Tom is wide-eyed with disbelief.

"Yes, but does it really matter where? Anyway, it was a dreadful mistake and I feel awful about it. So does Alex."

"Is that why they're splitting up?" Tom asks, putting everything together.

"No. I don't know. I don't think so. Annie says not."

"I can't believe she's still speaking to you."

"Well she wasn't, for a while. As you know. But she blames Alex for it. Thinks he took advantage of me while I was in a vulnerable position. With Mum and everything…"

"You don't agree?"

"No, not really. I'm a grown-up, aren't I? I was feeling sad – as we all were – and Annie had been being mean to Alex, as usual. I think we both needed some kind of comfort but obviously, clearly, that was completely the wrong way to find it."

Tom's mind is whirring. Whatever he'd expected, it wasn't this. He wants to call Cecily. Find out how she knew about this. Because surely, to have said what she did, she must have done. The pleasant, fuzzy feeling is gone, and all of a sudden he feels a bit sick.

"Are you alright, Tom?" Kitty asks.

"Yeah, great. I just found out my pregnant sister's husband cheated on her with our other sister."

"It wasn't like that, Tom," Kitty says warningly.

"Oh no?"

"No. And Annie wasn't pregnant then." Was she? Kitty isn't sure now. "And Alex didn't know she was pregnant. Not till last night."

"Fucking hell. So just you and Annie were in on it? She chose to confide in you, despite everything?"

192

"Tom," Kitty tries to put her hand on his arm but he shrugs her off. He does look pale, she thinks. Mavis runs up to them, barking. "It's OK," Kitty says to the dog. "Everything's OK."

"It's not though, is it?" Tom explodes. "It's not fucking OK! Mum's gone. Annie's pregnant. Alex and you are having an affair. And they're getting a divorce."

"Tom, calm down. Please. We're not having an affair. It was a kiss, just a kiss. I told you that." Kitty has adopted her no-nonsense older sister tone now. It does not go down well.

"Oh well that's fine, isn't it? That makes everything OK. And then you go and just fucking ignore us for weeks on end. While Dad's crying his heart out every night, and Annie's – well, Annie – and I'm just here trying to hold it all together."

"You've met Cecily though," Kitty offers gently, with a smile.

Cecily, Tom thinks. She knew about this too. But how? And why did she not tell him?

"I need some space. I need to walk," he says and stands up, calling to Mavis. "You'll be alright walking back from here on your own, won't you?"

Despite everything, he is concerned for his sister's safety, and I love him all the more for it.

"Yes of course, but Tom, don't go. Please. Let me walk with you. Let's talk."

"No, no, it's fine. I just need to get my head straight.

193

It's too much, and I shouldn't have been smoking, not after drinking at lunch as well."

"Tom," Kitty says quietly. "Do you hate me?"

"No, Kitty," he says sardonically, "I don't hate you, but I wish you'd bloody well pull yourself together. Sort it out, OK? Stop thinking about yourself all the time."

With these cutting – and really unwarranted – words, he calls to Mavis again, and he is gone. Kitty stands, feeling shaky, and watches until her brother has vanished around the corner. Then she walks back along the path, picking her way carefully around the worst bits of the mud, and emerges onto the path to the main road again. She shakes her head and blinks. She had not expected this to be the happiest birthday ever, but she had certainly not anticipated that it would be this awful.

20

Tom regrets the smoking, and the drinking, as he walks. Neither has been beneficial to him in terms of straightening out his thoughts, and he goes round and round his argument with Kitty, trying to remember what he said and thinking of a hundred different better ways he could have handled things.

But... Alex? Kitty and Alex? What the...?

It was just a kiss, though, he reminds himself – at least, if Kitty is to be believed. And Annie knows about it, and she seems to be fine with Kitty, so there is no good reason that he shouldn't be. But it all feels so messy. And dramatic. And stupid. And wrong.

Everything's just fucked since Mum died, he thinks. Except for Cecily, he reminds himself. Even Kitty had tried to make him think of Cecily, when he was mad at her. But then... Cecily... what had she said to him? *Don't be angry at Kitty, or Alex.*

How on earth did she know anything about this? Was she psychic? Or was she talking about something else? He had been annoyed at Kitty, he thinks, for not being in touch and not coming to visit, so maybe that's what she had meant. And Alex, well Annie had just announced they were splitting up, so perhaps that's where Cecily was going with that. Maybe she wasn't actually connecting the two names as she'd seemed to be. Still, it was a bit of a coincidence, wasn't it?

As he rounded the bend of the path away from one river and towards the other, he called Mavis to him. She came dashing over excitedly and then, seeing he had nothing for her, went rushing back off into the undergrowth. Tom pulled his phone from his pocket and called Cecily.

"Hello!" she answered after two rings, sounding happy to hear from him.

"Hi," he said, and doubted whether he should actually have this conversation – especially right now. But still, he had to know.

"Are you out with Mavis?" she asked. "I can hear the birds."

"Yeah," Tom said vaguely. "I was just with Kitty, but she's gone home now."

"Oh yeah?" She did know something. He could hear it in her voice.

"Yes. So she told me something... weird."

"Good weird?"

You know it wasn't, he thinks.

"No, I wouldn't say that. She said that something happened with her and Alex."

There was no reaction as there would have been if this was a surprise. In fact, Cecily didn't say anything.

"You knew, didn't you?"

"I – yes. But, well, I wasn't supposed to. I didn't want to. Oh god, Tom, I heard Kitty talking at the long barrow. I wasn't spying on her. I had just arrived, and I heard her voice and thought she was talking to somebody else. Well, she was. She was talking to your mum. As soon as I heard what she was saying, I left, and then – then I saw you."

"Me?"

"Yes. Remember, on New Year's morning?"

"When we saw the owl?"

"Yes." She sounds glum.

"You were trying to keep me away."

"Yes, I was, but…"

Suddenly that cherished memory, which had seemed to Tom an omen of a better year, is tarnished. She hadn't been trying to spend time with him, she'd just been trying to protect his stupid sister.

"Never mind," he says. "I've got to go."

"Tom…"

But he hangs up. He calls Mavis, more gruffly this time; not that she seems to mind, although she is a little bit miffed when she realises he is putting her back on her lead. Tom strides forward with purpose. His mind a swirling, whirling mess.

Oh Tom, I try to get through to him. *Just stop. Slow down. Think it through.*

But his drink-and-drug-misty mind is incapable of thinking anything through. All he wants to do is walk.

Mavis looks up at him but he's looking straight ahead. She trots along obediently at his side, in a way she had never done for me.

They traverse the slippery, muddy ditch and arrive at the path next to the other river, which is wider, and deeper, and faster-flowing than the first one. Tom stops for a moment, watching a stick caught up in an eddy underneath some tree roots. The water moves it round and round, like a cat playing with a mouse. Tom urges it to break free, to move on, but it appears to be doomed to this never-ending fate.

Mavis pulls at the lead. Tom takes the hint and walks on. He greets another dog-walker; a woman just a little younger than Graham and me, who sees only a pleasant-faced young man out for a Saturday afternoon stroll with his dog. She has no idea of the anguish he is in.

He carries on, and goes through a gate, along to the less well-trodden path now, which is boggy and difficult to traverse. Mavis follows him through, and the mud is up to her belly in places. She is muddy and bedraggled and looks like a different dog.

Tom picks his way to the edge near the river, where it looks a little firmer and he can use the trees to keep him steady – the other side of the path is bordered by a barbed-wire fence, and he doesn't fancy grasping onto that if he slips.

"Fucking hell," he mutters to himself.

Rarely have I seen my son in such a bad mood, but I

suppose these are extraordinary circumstances. I just wish he would stop, though. Take a breath. Think it through. Why exactly is he so upset about something which happened between his sisters? It doesn't involve him directly. It's not really Kitty he is angry at, or Alex, but he directs his feelings that way. Even towards Annie, for just apparently accepting what happened. Surely, surely her dumping Alex is tied up with this, even if she says it isn't. Annie is a proud person, thinks Tom, so maybe she's just saving face. How could she go on being married to a man who had tried it on with her sister?

Life's complicated, I try to tell him. *It's not black and white.* I wish he could hear me. He used to listen to me. We used to talk things through. It's no use, though.

Mavis spies a squirrel, and jerks the lead out of his hand. Tom, swearing, jolts forward, and catches his foot on a tree root. He reaches out for the nearest branch, to steady himself, but it's not strong enough. It snaps, and Tom finds himself in seeming slow-motion, unable to prevent the inevitable. He stumbles, slips, and slides down the riverbank. For a moment, he thinks his coat will save him, catching as it does on an overhanging branch but no, it rips, and he falls, into the cold, dirty water. Head-first. He could almost laugh, but his head hits a rock, and his mouth fills with water, and somewhere in the deep recesses of his mind comes a memory of being caught out by a wave, on a family holiday in Cornwall. He was four years old and he'd been tipped up, tossed about, panicking, while the water went over his head, but I'd seen him, and grabbed him, and pulled him out. He remembers it now, the sight of me in the bright summer light, his saltwater-sore eyes blinking and his mouth gasping, before bursting into shocked screams, his face drenched in tears.

It was nothing a cuddle and an ice-cream couldn't fix. I remember him, sun-warmed and wrapped in a towel, leaning against me, sand visible in amongst the roots of his damp, dark hair. I remember closing my eyes, and just feeling his presence there, and hearing the gulls, and the other beach-goers, and the girls chattering on behind us in the beach tent. Despite the mishap, that was a golden day.

Now, Tom is alone. Mavis, the little bugger, has gone careering off after that squirrel, and Tom, with a bleeding head and soaked to the skin, somehow manages to find the strength and the presence of mind to pull himself out of the water. He lies on the muddy bank, shrouded by trees and shrubs, panting and panicked, and suddenly, overwhelmingly tired. He'll just close his eyes for a moment, he thinks, before he goes to find Mavis.

Sometime later, the woman Tom had seen earlier is retracing her steps back home, having stopped at a friend's for a cup of tea.

She can see Mavis running back and forth through

the mud, churning it up even more. Is that the dog she saw earlier? She looks around for the young man but can see no sign of him – or anyone else, for that matter.

She puts her own dog back on his lead and walks towards Mavis, who she can see still has her lead attached. The woman moves cautiously, seeing that the dog is anxious.

"Hello," she says gently, and Mavis runs up to her, pushing her with her front paws, and then runs away again. "Are you OK?" the woman asks. She follows Mavis, trying to get hold of the lead but to no avail. "Where's your owner, eh?"

She looks around, further along the path, and across the fields, and can see nobody. Presumably the dog's managed to escape her owner and he's searching for her somewhere.

Luckily, she has a pocket full of dog treats. She calls to Mavis, and scatters some. Despite everything, Mavis is not one to turn down a piece of chicken, and she comes closer. The woman scatters some more, and manages to put her foot on Mavis's lead. She crouches to pick up the end of it, which is caked in mud. Then, offering more treats to Mavis, she moves back towards the main path, my beloved spaniel moving half-reluctantly with her, casting regular glances back over her shoulder.

When Mavis is calm, the woman asks her to sit. She crouches and looks for an ID tag but this has come off somewhere along the way. Thinking on her feet, the woman decides the quickest way to reunite dog and owner will be via Facebook.

She asks Mavis to sit again and, knowing more chicken is forthcoming, Mavis does as she is asked. "Good girl!" exclaims the woman, taking a couple of pictures with her phone and handing over her reward. Her own dog nudges her for his share, and she scatters some pieces of food on the ground for the two of them to find while she logs on to Facebook, finds the local community page, and posts the pictures, along with her phone number, and a description of where they found Mavis.

We'll take her back to our house and look after her until you can come and collect her, she types. *She's perfectly safe and well.*

That may be the case for Mavis, but Tom is now all alone on the riverbank, unconscious and becoming increasingly cold.

21

Oblivious to all this drama, Kitty has returned home. She had been tearful on the walk back, going over and over the argument with Tom, and engulfed by waves of fresh grief. Like her brother, she contemplates just how much else has gone wrong since I died. Not that I could have done anything to stop it, even if I'd been alive. But she is not to know that. To Kitty, it feels like my dying has torn her world apart, in so many more ways than she may ever have expected.

She thinks about calling Tom, and even calling Alex, but she pushes that thought firmly to one side. He has enough to worry about anyway.

By the time she reaches home, Kitty is feeling calmer and is determined to pull herself together for the sake of Graham.

"Worst birthday ever," she says to herself, as she goes through the garden gate. But, seeing her dad through the kitchen window, she plasters on a smile, and goes inside.

"No Tom?" Graham asks, while she is pulling off her boots.

"No, he carried on without me."

"Oh? Everything OK?"

"Of course. I'm just feeling a bit tired after the wine."

"Ah, yes, I know what you mean. You should have a rest, too. It's done me the world of good. Your sister's still asleep, as far as I know."

"And she didn't even have any wine!"

"No, but she's sleeping for two now, isn't she?"

Kitty smiles and hugs her dad. He has a little of the old Graham about him, she thinks. Maybe it's having all his children back together. Perhaps it's the thought of the new life coming into the family.

It is both those things, I know. And I also know there is even a little bit of pleasure at the thought that Annie has finally binned Alex; although Graham would never admit to this, of course. And he does realise that entering motherhood as a single parent isn't going to be easy but if anyone can pull it off, he thinks, it's Annie. And besides, he's around, with a lot of time on his hands. He can help out.

"I might take her a drink," Kitty says. "If she sleeps too long she might not sleep tonight."

"Good idea. Did she say she's off tea?"

"Yes, I think so. I'll take her a cold drink."

Kitty gets the lemon squash from the cupboard. It's what they always used to have when they were children. She pops some ice cubes into two glasses – she offers Graham one but he's making himself a coffee – and pours in the cordial then some water from the jug in the fridge. She takes a sip, then a gulp, realising how thirsty she is.

"Steady on!" Graham laughs as she downs her squash. "Leave some for Annie."

"I will!" She picks up her sister's glass and goes upstairs, knocking gingerly on the door.

"Mmmph," Kitty hears from inside. She pushes open the door and goes in. Annie is pulling herself up in bed, blinking her eyes open.

"How are you feeling?" Kitty asks.

"OK, I think."

"I brought you some squash."

"Thanks," Annie smiles. "Good walk?"

"Yeah, it was OK," says Kitty, not wanting to tell Annie about the argument just yet.

"Good."

Annie's phone pings. "Urgh. Alex, again."

"You can't really blame him," Kitty says, but stops herself saying anymore. She really shouldn't be standing up for her brother-in-law, given everything that's happened.

"Oh," Annie frowns, reading Alex's message.

"What?"

"He says Mavis is on the Facebook page, or something. Do you know what he's on about?"

Kitty's stomach lurches; a sudden, bad feeling hits her. "The local page? Let me see."

She reads Alex's WhatsApp, trying to ignore the earlier messages in the thread: **Hi, I thought you'd**

like to know a dog that looks like Mavis is on the Facebook page. Sure it's her. Take a look.

It's a fairly basic, slightly abrupt message, with no overtures of undying love, Kitty is pleased to note.

She pulls her own phone out – Annie is not on Facebook, of course. She searches for the local community page and yes, the first thing she sees is a post with two pictures of Mavis. Muddy, and grinning (or is she looking stressed?) but definitely Mavis.

"Shit."

She calls Tom. There is no answer. But maybe he doesn't want to talk to her. Still, if he's not with Mavis, he must be out looking for her.

"You call him," she says to Annie.

"Who?"

"Tom. He's not talking to me."

"What? Why not?"

"I'll tell you in a sec. Just give him a call and tell him we know where Mavis is. I'll message this woman to say we'll go and collect her."

Annie tries Tom's phone but again there's no answer. In fact, the phone is lying in the leaf litter by the river, having dropped from his pocket before he'd fallen into the water.

The woman from Facebook responds immediately. *Oh that's good news. She's a lovely dog, and having a great time with my lab but I'm sure she'll be happy to be reunited with you. Is your brother still out looking for her?*

I don't know, I haven't been able to get hold of him.

Oh, OK. Well I couldn't see him, I did look.

Where was Mavis when you found her?

Kitty feels her stomach twist, low down, as it does when she's worried or stressed.

She was running about in the mud, near the river.

The woman, whose name is Sandra, is worried now. What if something's happened to that nice young man? Why didn't she think to look a bit harder for him?

Shall I meet you, and show you where she was?

I don't want to put you to any trouble, messages Kitty.

You wouldn't be, honestly. I won't rest until I know he's OK anyway.

That's really kind of you.

Sandra and Kitty arrange to meet at the entrance to the river path.

"What's going on?" Annie asks.

"Hopefully, something and nothing," Kitty says. "But Tom's not answering his phone, and I just want to make sure he's OK."

"Why wouldn't he be?"

"He was upset. When he left me." As quickly as she can, Kitty fills Annie in on what happened.

"Oh bloody hell. I can't believe you two were smoking drugs!" Annie admonishes.

"I don't really think that's the key factor here, Annie," Kitty says.

"No, no, sorry." Annie swings her legs out of bed and pulls on a warm jumper.

"What are you doing?"

"I'm coming with you."

"But you're—"

"Pregnant?" Annie says derisively. "Yes, but I think I can just about manage a walk down the riverside."

"What about Dad?"

"Oh shit," Annie says. "We can't very well not tell him."

My daughters dash down the stairs and Annie lets Kitty do the talking.

"Dad, we need to get down to the woods," she says, trying to panic him as little as possible. While he had seemed on a slightly more even keel just now, like a sensitive horse it won't take much to spook him. "Somebody's found Mavis running in the woods, and we can't get hold of Tom. So we need to go and collect Mavis, and see if we can find Tom too. He's probably just looking for her," she tries to reassure him.

"What?" Graham, predictably, finds a range of terrible scenarios swimming before his eyes. It doesn't take much these days, for him to imagine the worst. In this case, however, he's not wrong.

The three of them pull on boots and hats and hop into Annie's car. She drives as quickly as she can to the little car park, and they see Mavis and a woman standing by the trees. Mavis is overjoyed to see them.

"Well, I can see you're not just trying to steal a strange dog," Sandra smiles, but she knows we need to get moving. "I'm so sorry, you know, that we didn't think to look harder for…?"

"Tom," Kitty says.

"Tom," she says his name, as if trying it out.

As they walk along the pathway, they decide to split into two pairs, Graham and Annie taking the main route along the side of the bigger river, while Kitty and Sandra follow the same route Kitty and Tom had taken earlier, taking Mavis with them.

Kitty and Sandra call Tom's name from time to time, stopping and pausing and listening. They hear Graham and Annie doing the same.

They see a man walking two greyhounds and ask if he's seen Tom but no, no luck.

As they approach the muddy ravine that Tom had crossed earlier, they see Graham and Annie up ahead.

"Any joy?" calls Graham, though he can clearly see that Tom is not with them and besides, Kitty would have called him and Annie if they had managed to find him.

My husband and my daughters are in high-alert, panic mode, but all are trying not to be, and all are trying not to worry the others too much. Sandra, meanwhile, is feeling awful. She has a son not much older than Tom, and a daughter a couple of years younger. She can very easily put herself in the place of this family. And she wonders briefly where the mother, the wife, is but thinks better of asking.

As they stride along the well-trodden path, and follow the curve of the river, Sandra says, "That's where she was." She points along to the place where she'd spotted Mavis.

Kitty and Annie run, as best as they can, through the churned-up mud. They pick their way carefully along the path and look back to Graham and Sandra, who are moving much more slowly towards them, Graham now holding Mavis's lead.

Phone him, I urge. *Phone him.*

"Let's try his phone again," Kitty says, and I marvel that she may actually have heard me, somehow. She pulls her phone out. Finds Tom's number and calls it.

"What was that?" Annie asks, putting her hand on Kitty's arm. They both hear it.

"It's over there!" Kitty says. She wades through the quagmire.

"Careful," says Annie.

"Don't worry."

Kitty sees the light of Tom's phone screen and her heart leaps for joy and then lurches with fear. If his phone is there but he isn't, where the hell is he? The rapid waters rushing just a metre or so below hold the answer, she is sure. And she can see, suddenly, a mark, all the way down the bank, where something – or somebody – has clearly slid down.

"Tom!" she calls desperately. "Tom!"

"Can you see him?" Annie's voice comes from above her.

Kitty turns, her face full of woe. "No," she sobs.

"Don't worry, don't panic," says Annie, her own face ashen. "Maybe he's just dropped his phone."

"But look," Kitty gestures to the marks Tom left on his way down the slope. And then Graham and Sandra and Mavis are there.

"You've found his phone?" Graham asks. All three of them jump to the worst conclusion. It isn't difficult for any of them to assume the worst has happened.

"Yes." Kitty holds it up.

"Oh God," says Graham. Then, "Mavis!" he snaps, as she pulls strongly on the lead, and he has to grab a tree trunk to stay upright. Still, she pulls.

"Hang on, Dad. Let me take her," says Kitty, and Graham carefully passes the lead down.

"Maybe let her go herself," Sandra suggests. "She could pull you in otherwise."

They all look at each other. Kitty unclips Mavis's lead, and she is off, pushing through the undergrowth, her tail wagging like mad. She stops just a few metres away, barking, and Kitty gingerly makes her way towards her. She sees it then, one of Tom's boots. Attached to one of Tom's legs. His dark, camo-colour clothing doing the job it was designed to do, he would have been very difficult to see if it weren't for the dog.

"Good girl, Mavis," Kitty says quietly and then calls back, "I think I can see him." And that's enough, for Graham and Annie to start sliding down towards her, and together they pull back the sharp, prickly shrubs and overhanging branches, to see a very pale, very wet Tom, soaked through and eyes closed, and dead to the world.

22

"Tom!" Graham had wailed, and it brought everything flooding back. The moment I'd left them, finally, and Graham's abject, guttural cry of grief. But in this moment there was no time to remember, or wallow in these memories.

Suddenly, Sandra was there, at their sides. "That's him?" she asked, even as she said the words knowing what a stupid question that was. "Can I have a look at him? I'm a nurse."

In another situation, Graham would have said. "My wife was a nurse," needing always to mention me. Wanting to talk about me, to tell people that I had died. However, this was not the time, and my husband and daughters stood back while Sandra moved towards Tom, and gently ushered away Mavis, who was licking his face, her tail going ten to the dozen.

"Can one of you get her back on her lead?" Sandra asked. I watched approvingly as she calmly and efficiently took charge of the situation.

Graham did as he was told, glad to have something to do. He called Mavis to him and got her to sit.

Meanwhile, Sandra checked for Tom's pulse. "He's alive," she said. "But he's very, very cold." She began taking her coat off, then wrapped it around his head, keeping his face uncovered. "We need to keep him warm. I need your coats. But I also need to phone for help. The ground's cold but I don't think we should move him, in case he's injured. Can you cover him, as well and as gently as possible? Be really, really careful with him."

Without hesitation, the girls and Graham pulled off their own coats, and lay them over Tom's body and legs while Sandra clambered up to the top of the bank, talking authoritatively to the emergency services.

"They're sending the air ambulance," she said.

And so they waited, holding Tom's cold hands and talking to him, begging him to wake up and look at them. The whole while, each of them talking to me in their heads, asking me to help if I possibly could. But I couldn't. All I could do was watch. And hope.

The air ambulance was there, landing in the nearby field, the paramedics running and making their way carefully through the barbed wire fence.

They took charge, Sandra giving as many details as she could, and moved Tom onto a stretcher, carrying him across to the helicopter and loading him up. Then, as fast as they had arrived, they were gone.

"Let me take Mavis," Sandra said. "She'll be safe with me, then you three can go straight to the hospital."

"Thank you so much," Kitty said as she, Graham and Annie began to make their way as fast as they possibly could back through the mud, tear marks tracking through the dirt on their faces.

Ignoring the puzzled looks of some passers-by, when they reached the smoother path they began to run, breathless but driven, leaping into Annie's pristine car, never minding the mud. Heart pounding, Annie drove them to the hospital, where they received a few curious looks. They pulled off their muddy wellies and walked quickly, trying not to slip on the clean, hard floor, until they reached A&E. Here, they were told that Tom was already being examined and that if they could just wait they would be seen as soon as possible, and given an update.

In silence, my husband and daughters sit, heads down, trying not to think the worst.

Why aren't you here, Ruth? Graham asks me again and again. As if I could make this any better. I couldn't.

"Shall I get us a drink?" Kitty asks, shivering despite the overbearing heat of the waiting room. It's something to do, she thinks.

She taps her card on the machine, gets two cups of coffee and one hot chocolate, and brings them back to their seats. The drinks are too hot but they clutch them for the physical comfort and warmth they provide.

And then, a nurse appears, and summons them.

"Is he — " Graham can't ask the question.

"He's alright," the nurse smiles. "He's conscious, and he's asking for you. And Mavis, who he tells me is a very naughty spaniel. He's very cold, and he has a nasty cut on his left leg, and a huge bump on the back of his head, but he's very much with us."

She grins, and Kitty bursts into tears. Graham puts his arm round her, though he is trying not to cry himself. Annie puts her hand to her belly, and thanks a god she doesn't believe in.

They are ushered through to see Tom, who is waiting to be taken to a ward. He's pale, and has a bruise on his forehead, and he's attached to a drip.

"Oh Tom!" Graham exclaims, and Tom accepts his hug, looking across to Annie and Kitty.

"I'm so sorry," Kitty says to him.

"No, I'm sorry," he says. "What an idiot."

"Mavis says she's sorry too." Annie smiles at him.

"OK, let's just agree we're all sorry."

"I'm not, I haven't done anything," says Annie, which makes Tom and Kitty laugh. Graham has no idea what any of them are talking about, but he doesn't care. He is just so grateful that he has his son.

The nurse comes back and ushers them out, saying they'll be moving Tom to a ward and they can see him properly once he's settled there.

"Fucking hell," Graham says, as they emerge outside, all in need of some fresh air.

"Dad!" Kitty says, mock-surprised.

216

"I think we're past the point of pretending we don't swear," he smiles. And he puts an arm around each of his daughters, pulling them in for a hug.

In front of them is the helicopter pad, where the air ambulance sits proudly, ready and waiting for its next rescue mission.

"Thank fuck he's alright," says Annie, relief making her unusually flippant.

"Too fucking right," Kitty replies, grinning irrepressibly.

"Happy fucking birthday," says Graham.

The three of them collapse with helpless laughter, their sides aching. Onlookers watch them with bemusement, amusement, and envy, but my husband and daughters are oblivious.

23

When Tom is settled in his room – an individual room off the main ward – the family are allowed to visit him, but not before a chat with one of the nurses.

"We'll be keeping him in for observation, probably just for one night," she says, in a reassuring tone, "but we are also keen that he sees a member of our mental health team."

The girls – as they will always be to me, no matter how old they end up – and Graham look at one another.

"Mental health?" Kitty clarifies.

"Yes. We—" she pauses, selecting her words. "We want to know how and why Tom went into the river as he did."

"He slipped," blusters Graham. "He told us. Tripped over a tree stump or something."

"Yes, that's what he's said to us too. And it's certainly been wet enough," she says, reverting to the British focus on weather in an attempt to bring them together.

"You think he went in on purpose?" Kitty asks.

Annie keeps quiet.

"He's told us about losing his mum. And some other issues," the nurse says.

"It's true, my wife died just a few months back," Graham says.

"I'm so sorry," the nurse says.

"But I don't know about any other issues. Well, apart from some changes in the family."

Annie looks at her dad, grateful for his sensitivity. "It's been a hard time," she says. "Mum was very ill, and it was all very sudden. And I'm in the process of splitting up with my husband; I suppose that might be an upset for Tom. He's known Alex since he was a young lad. It's a lot of change."

"Yes, and I've split up with my boyfriend," Kitty puts in. "Though I don't think Tom was that keen on him!"

I sense it all, this defensiveness in the three of them. They don't want this nurse to see their family as anything less than it is; close-knit but going through an incredibly difficult time.

"We love Tom!" Graham says now, and I can see he's fighting back tears.

"Mr Hebden," the nurse smiles a small, understanding smile. "I promise you it is just a precaution. We have to cover all the bases here, I am sure you understand. It will just be a chat with one of our team, to make sure there are no underlying issues. OK?"

"OK," Graham says, but his insides are churning, his emotions a tangle.

How I wish I could help him straighten them all out.

The girls, too, are mortified. What if...? But no. It couldn't be. He couldn't have. But what if...?

As a result, they go cautiously into Tom's room and are relieved to see it's just Tom there in the bed. There is nothing different about him, except for his pallor – although he's already regaining some colour in his cheeks – and the drip still attached to his arm.

"Hi," he smiles at each of them as they enter. As they sit, his face drops. "I'm so sorry," he says, and to their dismay he bursts into tears.

"Tom!" Kitty is the closest to him, and she reaches for him, gingerly, aware that she does not want to disturb the cannula or the tubing. "Don't be sorry."

"I am though! What an idiot. You must have all been so worried."

"Well we were, of course, but it's not like you did it on purpose." She hopes that's not saying too much. She checks his face for a reaction.

"No, but I left you on your own, didn't I? And I let Mavis go, and anything could have happened to her, and..."

"Son," Graham speaks loudly and surely. Kitty moves back to let their dad in. "Don't fret. Mavis is fine. We are all OK. No harm done, alright?"

I'm proud of him, for stepping in at exactly the right time. And I see some of the old Graham creeping back in. Always a dignified man, it's been painful to see him these last few months, crumbling and feeling utterly hopeless. Now, Graham is back, in this moment, at least.

Tom sniffs and tries to hold back his tears, but it's not easy.

"Perhaps it's too much, all of us being here," says Kitty. "What if Annie and I step outside for a while, and Dad stays for a bit? We can take it in turns sitting with you, Tom. We won't be far away."

"Actually," Tom says, "I'd like to talk to you, Kitty, if that's OK?" He is asking Graham and Annie as much as Kitty.

"Of course," they all murmur, eager to placate him.

"Dad and I can go and find a vending machine," Annie says. "Is there anything you'd like, Tom?"

"I actually–" he says, almost sheepishly – "keep thinking about Maltesers."

"Really?" Kitty laughs. "Are you allowed them?"

"I don't know. I don't think I'm nil by mouth or anything."

"Tell you what, we'll see what we can do, and you can always ask the nurse or the doctor when they're next in."

Kitty smiles as her sister and dad leave the room, then she turns to Tom. She is nervous, fearing that he's about to lay into her again.

"I'm so sorry," he says. "What an idiot. I shouldn't have said all that to you. I shouldn't have stormed off."

"Don't worry," she says, the nurse's words ringing

in her ears – *We want to know how and why Tom went into the river as he did* – "about anything."

"Yes, but I was just being a knob. God, I know there's nothing between you and Alex. And I know strange things happen sometimes, especially when people are under extreme stress, and grieving."

His eyes start to well up again and Kitty finds hers doing the same.

"Tom," she says, bravely, but determined to discover the answer. "What happened?"

"What? When?"

"When you fell in. You did fall in, didn't you?"

"You've seen how wet my clothes were! Of course I fell in," he says, then it dawns on him what she is actually asking. "Oh my god, Kitty, yes, it was an accident. Of course. Shit, if I had anything else in mind you don't think I'd try and do it in that poxy river, do you?"

He laughs now, and Kitty can't help joining him. She is shaking though, her pent-up nerves getting the better of her.

"You didn't really think… did you?"

"Well no, I didn't. But I think the hospital staff are worried about you."

"Oh I know," he says breezily. "I was a bit of a mess earlier, and blurted it all out. Even about you and Alex, I'm so sorry. And Mum, of course."

"Of course."

"I wish she was here, so much. Do you?"

"Every day."

"She'd have got all this straightened out in no time."

"To be honest, Tom, I don't think any of this would have happened if she was still here."

Those are some hard words to hear. If I was still there. And she's right, very possibly. If I hadn't got ill, if I hadn't died, life might look very different for them all. Annie and Alex might still be muddling along, and I am quite sure Alex and Kitty would never have looked at each other the way they have found themselves doing. But then, it's possible that on a different trajectory, Annie may not have become pregnant. And Tom may not have met Cecily – although, with her working at the pub, I'm quite sure that one way or another those two would have found each other. If I hadn't died, then, some things would be better but maybe some things would be worse. It's all theoretical anyway, and it's life (and death).

"No," Tom looks pensive. "No, you're probably right. Would you still be with Olly, do you think?"

"I don't know about that!" she laughs. "And you know, maybe it would all have happened exactly as it has, regardless."

"Predeterminism?"

"Something like that. But I know that might sound like I'm making excuses. What happened with me and Alex was nothing; a stupid, fleeting moment, but still it happened, and I was a part of it, and that was my choice. I don't hold anyone else to blame for my actions."

"I know. But you're upset as well, Kitty. Mum… Olly…"

"Yes, but I'm still a responsible adult!"

"That's debatable."

She mock-cuffed him around the ear and they grinned at each other, and I felt myself settle a little.

"Anyway, sis, it was stupid of me to react like I did. You and Annie have clearly sorted things out and really it's none of my business. I suppose I'm struggling with all this change. I just wish – I wish things could go back to how they were."

"I know. Me too. Well, in some ways. But we have to go with it, Tom. Remember Mum said life goes on? And it does. We might not feel like it should, but it has to." Kitty has tears rolling down her cheeks now and she takes her brother's hand. "God, Tom, it's shit, isn't it? Everything can feel normal for a moment and then you just remember…"

"Yep. Exactly that."

"But I'm so glad I've got you, and Annie, and Dad. We'll get through it you know, all of us. People do."

"But how?" he asks, so utterly hopelessly.

"Well, for you, Cecily might be a part of it."

"Maybe."

Kitty is surprised by this but doesn't feel justified in questioning her brother about his relationship, when he is in full possession of the facts about how messed up she is in this respect. All she says is, "I hope so." She leaves it at that.

In the end, Tom in in hospital for two nights. He has a locker stacked with Maltesers, and Minstrels, and flapjacks, as Graham went a bit over-the-top at the vending machine, so Tom has an impressive array of snacks to offer visitors. Graham, Annie and Kitty are in and out, and Alex also comes to see him.

Tom is sorry to see how sad his brother-in-law looks. Despite his poking fun at Alex, he is very fond of him deep down and remembers when he was a teenager, and Alex first came into their lives, how Alex would spend time with him and humour his incessant talk about the latest band he was obsessed with, or book he was reading.

"Flapjack?" Tom asks, rooting around in his bedside locker.

"Thanks," Alex says, barely registering what he is doing as he peels away the plastic wrapping and bites into the too-sweet, sawdusty cake.

"I'm sorry, man," says Tom. This, at least, makes Alex smile.

"No worries," he says. "Well, not really. But it's not for you to be sorry."

"I know, but…"

"I know. I can't believe it," Alex munches away despondently, sending a shower of crumbs scattering across the otherwise spotless floor.

Tom doesn't know what to say. Having questioned

Annie, he knows her mind is made up. There is no point in giving Alex false hope, suggesting that they may yet get back together.

"But you're going to be a dad," he says, wondering even as the words come out whether this is going to be a comfort.

"Mental," Alex says, still staring at the floor.

"But good?" Tom asks, his eyes on his brother-in-law.

"Well, yes…" Alex lifts his head a little. "In other circumstances…"

"But even in these circumstances," Tom says. "You're going to be a dad. A dad, Alex. And do you know what, I think you'll be a great one."

My god, Tom, I think, *how do you do it? How do you find it within you to offer such comfort when you're feeling so awful yourself?*

"Do you?" Alex looks straight at Tom now. "Really?"

"Yes. Really. And I know you won't be together in the same house as the baby, and that must be a hard thought."

"Just a bit," Alex says, but I can see Tom's words have genuinely cheered him, if only a little, and if only for a moment.

"But, for all Annie is – well, Annie – you know she's a fair person. Scrupulously so, sometimes. She's not going to be one of those people who messes their ex about, or their kid. She's…"

Tom trails off, hoping he's right. That Annie won't

shut Alex out and away from his child.

"No, I know. We've already talked about it, a lot. She wants me to be involved, and we're even thinking in the early days that I might move back in, for a bit, so we can both share the load, so to speak."

"Wow, well that's good, isn't it?" Tom asks. He is starting to feel tired now. He's already given a lot.

"Yes it is, Tom. It is, mate. Thank you." Alex crumples up his wrapper. "Now, any fit nurses here?"

"Alex," Tom says, rolling his eyes.

"I'm thinking for you, not me!" Alex protests. "Although, I did hear you might have a girlfriend. Cecily, from the long barrow?"

"We've seen each other a few times," Tom says, giving nothing away.

"Well that's great. She's lovely. Perfect for you."

"Maybe," Tom says, and my heart sinks.

"I hope so," says Alex, in an unwitting echo of his sister-in-law's words.

Tom has been reluctant to see Cecily while he's in hospital, but she is so persistent that he eventually gives in.

I'll be home tomorrow, he'd messaged her. **I'll be in touch then.**

I'd love to see you before then though, she had replied. **If it's OK with you.**

Sure, he'd said, **Come this afternoon, I'll tell Dad and the sisters not to bother.**

Great. Can't wait to see you xx

He hadn't replied. *Tom, what are you doing?*

Cecily arrives, looking pink-cheeked and slightly shy. Tom too is feeling self-conscious, in his pyjamas and sitting in one of those high-backed chairs they have. Perhaps this was why he didn't want her to come – embarrassment – but no, I know it's more than that.

"How are you?" She doesn't know whether to hug him, or kiss him, and opts instead to hand him a brown paper bag of grapes. "I got you these," she says. "It's traditional, isn't it? Grapes for hospital patients, I mean."

Tom opens his locker, gesturing to the still impressive pile of snacks contained within. "It's nice to see some fresh fruit, after all this," he smiles.

"Blimey. Have you been raiding the vending machine under cover of darkness?"

"It's mostly courtesy of Dad," he says. "And the Dairy Milk's from Alex." He watches her reaction as he says his brother-in-law's name.

"He's come to see you?"

"Yeah, well, you know, I'm like his brother, aren't I? And I've known him a long time."

Cecily hears what she is meant to in those words. She hasn't known Tom all that long. She isn't part of his world in the way that his brother-in-law is – even though she knows full well that Tom finds Alex more than a little irritating. It's Tom himself who has told her this. But suddenly she feels like he is putting her on the outside.

"It's nice he came," she says.

"Yeah. He's properly broken, though. Annie… the baby…"

"I was thinking about that. It must be really hard for him," she says.

"You think?" Tom himself doesn't fully understand why he is being like this. But at some very deep level he feels betrayed by Cecily. It may not be logical, but it's how he feels, and he's having a tough time fighting it. She was meant to be for him, though; his person, his possible partner, but she's been keeping this really quite important secret from him. Yes, he knows it's not her secret to tell. And yes, he can see why she didn't say anything; he even knows that he very likely would have made the same choice, in that situation. But that morning; that owl on New Year's Day. It had felt magical, to him. Like a turning point, and a good omen, for a better year. It's tainted now, with the knowledge that she was just trying to distract him, and keep him away long enough for Kitty to make her confession and make her escape.

No, it's not logical, in any way, but I remember how it is in a new relationship, and how everything seems so full of meaning and passion and emotion. When somebody matters so much to you, it's easy to fear the worst. And now Tom, in his own fear, having been deeply hurt and heartbroken once already within the previous year, is trying to protect himself from going through more pain again.

He sighs now. "Cecily," he says.

No, she thinks. She knows what is coming.

No, I think as well. *Don't do it, Tom. You are not thinking straight.*

She looks at him directly. She has courage. I hurt for her.

"I think we should stop seeing each other," Tom says, feeling like a knife is piercing his heart.

"Can I ask why?" Oh, to have had as much self-control and dignity as this young woman, when I was her age.

"I just – I think it's the wrong time. I'm not over what's happened with Mum. I can see that so clearly now. I thought I had it under control, and I obviously don't."

"It's a long road," Cecily says. "You might not ever be over it, as such. It's just awful, Tom. I'm so sorry."

He's doubting himself now. Kicking himself, in fact.

Can he really let her go, this beautiful, caring young woman? But equally, can he trust himself at the moment? And can he trust her?

Yes, he thinks, it's ridiculous to think that he can't. OK, she didn't tell him about Kitty and Alex, but he does get that, really. But it's made him question everything. And his head is a mess. He knows it is. No, he thinks, he is right. Now is not the time.

"It's not your fault," he says now, slightly gruffly. "Mum, I mean. Or any of this," he says.

"I'm so sorry as well, though, about that morning. About Kitty, and…"

"I know, I know. I would have probably done the same in your situation. But I just thought, well I felt, we were getting close."

"We were!" she says, using every fibre of her being to prevent herself sounding desperate. "We are. But it, it wasn't my secret to tell."

"No, I can see that. I do know that. I'm just a mess, Cecily. I'm sorry. My family's falling apart and I don't know how to deal with it all."

"I can see that," she says sadly. "I understand." And she kisses him on the cheek. "Take care of yourself, Tom. You know where I am."

Cecily is not the only person leaving the hospital in tears, and Tom is not the only patient crying quietly to himself. I sit quietly beside him as he cries and questions the wisdom of what he's just done, looking ahead to a future which seems like a gaping black cavity now that he's wilfully, stubbornly – and, in my opinion, stupidly – extinguished his bright ray of hope.

24

"I'm exhausted," I say to Teresa, and Kiran, who sit either side of me. "I would never have imagined that as a possibility. I thought it was only for the living."

"It's not that straightforward, is it?" Kiran motions for me to lean on her. I do, gratefully.

"What's it all about?" I ask, not really expecting either of them to know the answer.

"It's hard," Teresa says. "So hard. But I think it's about letting go. Remember when your children were small – when they first went to school, or nursery? That feeling of handing them over, entrusting your most precious people in all the world to strangers. I think of it like that now. We've done our bit; played our part. There is very little more we can do now but watch and try, somehow, to reach them when they really need us. In time, I think, they come to need us less. And that's when we can begin to loosen our grip."

"I think Teresa's right," says Kiran. "And that in itself is a scary prospect. Considering that these people who have always relied on us, always turned to us, begin to find other pathways to follow. It's hard to accept. But all of those who have gone before us have been through the same thing. My parents. Your parents. We know they're still with us, and always have been, but at some point in our lives on Earth, we had to live without them. Rely on ourselves more."

"Not me," Teresa says cheerfully. Her mum is still in a nursing home, healthy and happy, though 'a couple of rounds of sandwiches short of a picnic', as Teresa puts it.

"I was awful after Mum and Dad died," I say, "but the children were young and so I had to carry on."

"And it probably took you a lot longer to process your loss," Kiran says gently. "I was the same – caught up in homework and school uniforms and getting them to Brownies, or Guides, or piano, or swimming."

"You were one of *those* parents," Teresa says knowingly.

"Yes," Kiran says, not taking offence. "I was. I felt like I would be letting them down if they weren't constantly occupied, and busy and sociable, and developing new skills."

"Well, we packed Derek off to boarding school at a tender age, and I was required to host dinner parties for my dreadful ex-husband's colleagues, all the while wishing I just had my little boy home and that I could curl up with him, reading his bedtime story."

"That must have been hard," I say.

"It's all hard, isn't it? But sometimes it's as hard as you let it be. Life is messy, there's no getting around

234

it. But it got a whole lot better once I left that life and found Val."

This makes me smile. Kiran, too.

"I'd never have guessed you were such a romantic, Teresa."

"It's nothing to do with romance! Well, not really. It's just when you know something is right…"

"She does seem like quite an incredible person."

"Oh, she is. And I am so very grateful Derek has her now. His father is useless."

"How was Derek," I ask, thinking of Tom, "at first, I mean?"

"After I died?" she asks, airily. It always seems strange to hear those words from one of my long barrow family, because we may have all died, but actually here we still are. I still have an awful lot to get used to with all this.

"Yes."

"He was a mess. Such a state. Honestly, your lot – and yours, Kiran – are handling things so much better."

"Really?"

"Yes, really. My boy, well he just went into overdrive with work, and when he wasn't working he was out drinking and doing all sorts. Honestly, I had to turn away sometimes. It was unbearable. He was driving himself into the ground. Val could see it. She was grieving herself, of course, but she still never took her eye off him. She bided her time, sensible woman that she is, and one day when he was being sick in the kitchen sink, she waited till he'd finished and then she sat him down and gave him a proper talking to. I was so proud. 'Look, my love, you don't need to do this to yourself,' she said. 'You're messing yourself up and you're wasting your young life.' Implicit was that I would not have approved, but she never said that directly. 'Throwing up in the kitchen sink!' Val said to him, and for some reason that hit exactly the right note. He looked at the sink, and remembered me being there, filling the kettle, or rinsing the crockery. I was with him, of course, trying to breathe some sense into him, and all of a sudden, it just came. His head was pounding and his stomach was aching, and all of his sadness found its way out. He was crying, and sobbing, and rocking, and Val took him in her arms and she held him for ages." Teresa's far away now as she remembers this scene. "Just ages. And I wished it could be me there, doing that. I wished I could hold him, and comfort him, and that I was not the source of his sadness."

We are all quiet now, contemplative. Then Teresa smiles. "But look at him now. He and Val. How far they've come! She was a mess that night, after Derek had gone to bed, early, and she was left awake and restless and utterly drained, tossing and turning in our bed. In the morning, he slept for hours, and that was some relief to Val. I remember she sat in one of the comfy chairs in the breakfast room, a strip of sunlight falling on her, her mug of tea cooling in her hands, and I sat with her, trying so hard to soothe her, and to thank her, for looking after my son when I couldn't. She fell asleep, her mug near enough still full, and she nearly spilled it over herself but – and this I was very proud of – I managed to warn her. I whispered to her, and she awoke just enough to realise what was happening, and she put that cup down, then she closed her eyes again, and she nodded off, thinking she had just dreamed of me. I only wished I could have put a blanket over her. Tucked her in. But she was OK. She was good. She was resting."

"It sounds like that was a turning point," Kiran says.

"Yes, but as you know, it's not that straightforward. You think they've cracked it, then they slip back again."

"That sounds about right," I say, feeling very much like the new girl.

Kiran smiles. "It's like Teresa says. Part of our – I hesitate to say 'journey', but you know what I mean – part of what we have to do now, I think, is to let them go, and learn to be for ourselves. Just as those we've left behind have to learn to live without us. It doesn't mean we have to leave them, ever, but it's a matter of acceptance, and looking around. Looking ahead."

We are alerted to the presence of somebody approaching the barrow. There are footsteps and the sound of voices, approaching.

Teresa smiles. "I knew they'd come!"

Of all our visitors, Val and Derek are the most frequent. Tom was giving them a good run for their money but I feel like, given the state of things with Cecily, he may be here a little less from now on. It doesn't matter; I can see him anyway, but I must admit it's felt nice knowing that he has been coming here to visit me.

Derek and Val giggle as she tries to put the code into the lock.

"Here, let me do it, Sausage Fingers!" Derek laughs.

Teresa is smiling but a little sadly. "It's arthritis," she says. "Poor Val. It's really making her feel her age."

Kiran and I look at each other. "I suppose at least we never had to feel like that," I say.

"True. Always a silver lining!" Kiran says. "Look, let's go outside, shall we? Leave Teresa to her visitors."

Outside is glorious. It's an early spring day, the trees are in bud, the birds are in song, and the fields which until this point have been brown and flat and often waterlogged have soaked in all the rain and are now sporting a short green stubble as the new growth begins to push through.

We are quiet together, letting it all sink in. Feeling the warmth of the sun's rays. Watching the flock of tiny long-tailed tits flit across the almost-cloudless sky. It fills me with joy, and thoughts of my family's turmoil begin to find the right place within me. I will not, cannot, ever stop caring, but I have to accept I can do nothing but be with them. I have to trust they will find their way.

At the sound of more footsteps, I turn and see that Kitty is coming, and I'm delighted to see her. She has not been here for quite some time. She should have been back at work by now, but Meg has insisted she stays here with Graham, and Tom, and Annie, for the week.

"It sounds like they need you," Kitty's boss said to her. "The dogs and I will manage. Which is not to say we could manage without you forever. But go on, I think you need this as much as your family does. Stay a few days until it's all come right."

"I just hope it does," Kitty said.

"It will," Meg smiled down the phone. "Your family is special. They're close in a way mine has never been. You'll get there."

"Thank you, Meg."

"No worries."

Now, with Tom back home, and seeming more steady, Kitty has taken the chance to come out to the barrow. And yes, here comes Mavis, and she's heading straight for me, her tail up and her tongue lolling out of the side of her mouth. She jumps at me and I am overwhelmed. She's seen me, I am sure of it. How I wish I could scoop her up and return her greeting.

I crouch and she runs rings around me, her whole body wagging along with her tail.

Kitty, who of course cannot see what Mavis is making such a fuss over, laughs. "Crazy dog!" she says. She, my middle child, is feeling full of the beauty of this day, and also relief that things are settling with Annie, and Tom, and that everyone (except Graham, that is), knows what has happened, and yet nobody hates her.

She feels bad for Alex, and worse for Cecily. Tom has made a huge mistake there, she thinks, but now is not the time to talk to him about all that. He needs to get back to basics and sort himself out. She is sure that he is telling the truth, that he did not go into the river on purpose. He was not trying to end his life. She's right, as well, but I can see why she might be worrying otherwise.

Even so, he's not in a good way. As she approaches the barrow, she thinks of how he has always, almost too easily, breezed in, and collected my urn, as if it's the most natural thing in the world. While Derek and Val, who right now are emerging with Teresa's urn, are able to do this matter-of-factly, it's been far too much too soon for Tom, and Kitty – who has never felt comfortable with it – is relieved to realise this. She's felt like she's not been strong enough or grown-up enough. Now she knows Tom was really in denial.

"Hello!" Val greets Kitty and Mavis turns, running across to say hello as well.

"Hi," Kitty says. "How are you?"

"We are very well thank you, aren't we, Derek?" Val turns to Teresa's son, who is just behind her, blinking as he comes out into the full daylight.

"What? Oh yes, hi," Derek says. "Beautiful day."

"It really is," Kitty beams. She has not felt this good, she considers, for – well, she can't actually remember when she last felt this good.

"We were going to have a coffee," Val says. "Sit in the sun for a bit. Care to join us?"

"Oh, erm…"

"No pressure, of course."

"No, no, that would be lovely. If you're sure."

"Of course. Did you want to go in first, though?"

"Yes, I was just going to tie Mavis up."

"Why don't we look after her?" Val suggests. "Derek, you give me that–" Derek hands the urn over, obediently – "and you can get the dog back on her lead, dear, and Derek can take her. He loves dogs but we can't have one, I'm allergic."

"Oh, are you? I don't think she should come with you, then, don't worry –"

"No, allergic to the mess, I mean," Val laughs. "I may not look it but I'm disgustingly house-proud."

"It's true," says Derek. "The only pet I could get away with is one of those bald cats."

"Or a naked mole rat?" Kitty suggests.

"I hadn't thought of that. Perfect!" Derek grins.

"Over my dead body!" Val shivers.

Kitty smiles to herself as she enters the long barrow. Derek and Val have lit a few of the candles, including the one in front of my niche.

"Hi Mum," Kitty murmurs, feeling slightly self-conscious in the knowledge that Derek and Val are not far away. "How are you?" Now she feels really stupid. But she perseveres. It's meant to be good to talk to us, the dead ones, she's been told, as though we are still here. *I am!* I say to her. *I'm always here. Always with you. If only you knew.*

"I'm sorry I haven't been for a while. It's all been, well it's all been a mess. I'm embarrassed as much as anything, Mum. Ashamed, too. This should never have happened." Even as she says this, she wonders if that is true. Is all this in fact exactly what should have happened? "Anyway, it all seems to have settled now, a bit. Tom's home, safe and dry. It was scary, though, Mum. I thought something terrible had happened to him. It very nearly had. And now he's gone and ended things with Cecily, and I think he's mad, but maybe they'll work it out. I wish they would. Annie and I might not have done very well with our choices but Tom's found his perfect woman, I'm sure of it. I wish you were here, to talk some sense into him." She is quiet for a while. "Do you know what, Mum? It's made Dad a bit better. This thing with Tom, I mean. And maybe it's the thought of being a grandad, too. I don't know. He just seems a bit more... present... again. I hope so, anyway. I think I've been missing him as much as you. Not as much, that's stupid, but it does feel like he's been absent." Kitty lets her tears come now, but not for long. "God, Mum, it's all so hard. And I do wonder sometimes what the point of it all is. Not that I don't want to live, nothing like that. But what is the point? We live, we mess things up, we're all a bit selfish. I just don't get it. But then I come here, on a beautiful day, and it reminds me that I can love life. I don't know."

She hunches forward, her head resting on her hands. I want her to sit back, roll her shoulders. Relax. I try to wreathe myself around her, breathe into her. *It's OK, Kitty. It's all OK. I don't know life's secrets any more than you do, but I promise there will be happiness again. I know there will.*

She sits, and then she hears Mavis's yap from outside. "I'd better go, Mum. I won't bring... you..." she is still not sure of this, when it comes to the urn, and she's right. It's not me in there. It's just ashes.

She stands, and as she does she rolls back her shoulders. There is a satisfying click as she does so, as if something has slotted into place, and I wonder if maybe, just maybe, I have got through to her somehow.

When she steps outside, the world seems more alive, and Derek releases Mavis so that she can run to Kitty and she does, greeting her as if it's been years.

"I'll pour your coffee now!" Derek calls from the bench. "I didn't want it to get cold."

"Thank you," Kitty calls back. She half-jogs across, Mavis dancing around her ankles. When she reaches the bench, Val stands to make space for her. Kitty protests.

"No, I need to stretch my legs," says Val. "My hands are already like claws. I need to make sure my legs at least keep on working."

Kitty sits and Mavis puts her chin on her knee.

"She's such a lovely dog," Derek says. "I wish Val would cave in. Or I could get my own place of course," he says wryly. "I am thirty-six, after all."

"Nearly grown up!" Kitty grins.

"Getting there. I had been saving, for my own place. I was travelling for a while, then came back to Mum and Val's, and I was thinking of moving on, maybe a city for a while – Manchester, or Leeds, maybe Bristol – but then Mum got ill."

"And your whole world changed."

"Yep."

"It's just unreal, isn't it?"

"It is. Still, sometimes. It's been years now. But she's still right here." He presses his hand on his heart. Teresa, next to him, puts her hand on his.

"It's so hard. And I never quite knew, till it happened to me."

"No, well, you don't, do you? It's like so many things, I suppose. I've definitely lost friends because they just haven't got it. Barely asked how she was when she was ill. Sent a card when she died. Moved on. I think they think I should have done, too."

"I don't think you can ever move on from losing your mum. Not if you're lucky enough to have had a good one."

"No. What was your mum called?"

"Ruth."

"Of course. That's right."

"And your mum was Teresa?"

"Yes."

"To Teresa and Ruth." Kitty raises her plastic coffee cup, and Derek mirrors her.

"To Ruth and Teresa." Their eyes meet across the rims of their cups as they drink the toast. Teresa and I look at each other and smile.

25

Back at the family home, Tom is lying on the sofa, thinking about how it was when he was ill, off school, and he'd be in that very spot, tucked in under his duvet, the TV on and me busying myself around the house, making the most of an unplanned day off work. It was always me who'd take the time off – funny, really, but it just wasn't the done thing for a man to take a day off because their child was ill; often, the mother would not be working anyway but if, as in my case, a woman had a job and children, it would be her job that had to take the hit. Her work, her career. I am not sure how much things have really changed since then to be honest, and I wonder how Annie is going to manage this. What would I be doing, if I was there with her now? Would I be pushing her to think ahead to these eventualities? Might I even be encouraging her to get back with Alex, just to make life easier? I realise that it is quite likely I'd be doing exactly that. Purely out of worry for her taking on all this responsibility herself but I see clearly now that a half-baked relationship is not the key to happiness. Besides, it seems like she and Alex are working together on this, even if they are no longer a couple. It is far from easy, but they are looking for the best way forward.

Tom, meanwhile, has regressed. I can feel it. Perhaps more accurately, it's caught up with him, finally. My illness, my death. Everything that came with those two things. Those moments and details which will stay with him forever, but which go unseen by the outside world.

I used to think about this, when my own mum became ill and died. The news you share with your friends, and your colleagues: "Mum died." It's a simple fact and seems very straightforward, but the depths hidden beneath those two short words... Everything that came before that moment of death, and everything that has come afterwards. The conversations, tears, irritations; arguments, even. Restless, sleepless nights. Stressful, anxiety-riddled dreams. Moments of blissful forgetting, for a moment, then the remembering hitting harder than ever. Waves of disbelief, self-doubt. Panic.

Tom, these last few months, has been trying his best to bypass it all. To willingly, wilfully, accept the fact that I have died. Death, he says to anyone who will listen, is something that people should talk about more. We need to be more open about it. He's right, but that doesn't detract from the feelings of grief and bereavement and unbelievable loss.

His fall, and subsequent near-death experience, have shaken him and also brought it all forward, all that he has tried to brush aside. It's hard to see him going through this, but it's necessary.

Mavis, of course, keeps him company, delighting in the extra-cosy duvet she can snuggle into, tucking herself into the curve Tom's body makes.

Mavis was absolutely fine after her little adventure. Sandra kept her for two days in the end and she and Mavis, and her own dog, Troy, have formed quite a bond.

When Graham and Kitty went to collect Mavis, Sandra invited them in, and they ended up telling her our family's story, this last year (leaving out the part about Kitty and Alex, which Graham of course is not privy to anyway).

"She was nice," Graham said as they drove away, having promised to meet up to get the two dogs together again. "I feel bad for going on about your mum, though. And telling her about Annie and the baby, too. 'Airing our dirty washing', my mum would have said."

"Ah no, she was happy to listen, I think. And it's good sometimes to talk to somebody unconnected with it all. I know I haven't been around so much lately, Dad, but I don't think that's one hundred percent a bad thing. It's so hard. We're so close, as a family, but sometimes it feels like if we spend too much time together, we might never move on. Not move on. I don't mean away from each other, and I don't mean away from Mum, but maybe we feed into and off each other's grief. Oh, I don't know." Kitty felt her cheeks growing red as she glanced at her dad, who seemed not to be listening, his eyes on the road. Maybe she was talking nonsense. She has to second-guess herself a lot these days. Nothing seems real, sometimes. It was quite possible she was just losing touch with reality. But then Graham looked at her.

"You're very wise, Kitty, do you know that?"

Yes! I wanted to shout. *Graham, that is exactly the right thing to have said!*

"I don't know about that," Kitty said, but she was pleased.

"No, love, you are. I hadn't thought of it like that at all. I've just wanted to be with you and your brother and sister. You're the ones who loved your mum as much as I did, and I don't have to pretend to be anything with any of you. But maybe that's not fair on you, anyway. I should be being your dad. Looking out for you. Your relationship's broken down, and now Annie's too, and you're both just getting on with it."

"But that's OK, Dad," Kitty said gently. "These are our decisions, and we are adults, you know."

"Yes, I know, but I'm still your dad." Graham's hands tightened on the steering wheel briefly. "You are right, Kitty, about us not becoming insular. Your mum wouldn't, would she?"

"No, I don't suppose so. But you never know what somebody will be like in this situation."

"I do," Graham said firmly. "She'd have been looking for ways to help other people. That was her, wasn't it? She did genuinely always want to help people, but it was also a good way of keeping herself from letting things get to her. It's why she went back to work after she was ill, when you were all little."

"That must have been hard," said Kitty.

"Like you wouldn't believe." Graham kept his eyes on the road, remembering those awful months when I'd been ill that first time, and he'd been racked with guilt over his affair. He was right, about my going back to work being a kind of therapy for me. There, in the hospital, I could look after other people. I could see people in pain and sometimes help to make them better; and if they could not be made better, I could at least help make things easier. Having been through illness myself, I could empathise, but I was also hurting so badly from feeling betrayed. And I was becoming aware that the last few years of my life had been all about my family.

In becoming a wife, I had taken on Graham's needs, anxieties and problems as though they were my own. In becoming a mother, I had given myself physically, emotionally and mentally. My thoughts at home were full of the children, and what they needed each day. At work, despite the fact that it was another draw on my reserves of energy, and again required me to be thinking of others, it was also a place, and a time, for me. And I felt appreciated.

I could be neat and orderly – in fact, I had to be. I could be an adult, with colleagues, and friends, and people who listened to me. Respected me. If a work situation had been very hard, or a patient had been difficult, there were people to talk to. A manager concerned for my welfare. I was perhaps given even more attention, as I was still deemed to be recovering from illness, and I must admit I liked it.

I never thought Graham realised any of this. I thought he just considered it a job, but it seems that he understood more than I ever knew.

Graham comes into the lounge with some cheese on toast, and a cup of tea. Mavis's head goes up, her nose sniffing the air.

"Think you can sit up, Tom?" Graham asks his son.

Tom shuffles around, his hair sticking up and his face pale. He pushes the duvet down. "Thanks, Dad," he says, managing a smile.

"No problem. I hope you're hungry. You need building back up."

Tom takes a bite. *Not bad.*

"This came for you," Graham says, handing Tom an envelope. He knows who it's from, as does Tom, who takes it and puts it to one side.

"Aren't you going to open it?"

"In a bit. I'll eat this first."

"Alright. Want me to sit with you?"

"Sure."

Graham pushes some of the duvet away and sits next to Tom. They watch an antiques programme together, making derisive comments about the presenter.

Graham is glad to see some real colour is beginning to touch Tom's cheeks again. "How are you feeling?"

"Oh, you know…"

"I don't, really. I've never fallen in a river, or had hypothermia. I am worried about you, Tom."

"You don't need to be," Tom says uncomfortably.

"No, I do. I really do. And I feel awful, that you've had to carry me through these last few months since your mum died. Your sisters have been great but you've been… well, you've been here. Every day. You've seen me at my worst, Tom, and I'm sorry about that."

"Don't, Dad."

"No, it needs saying. It's my turn to help you now. But you'd better make the most of it, before Annie has that baby, because god knows she's going to need a hand then!"

This makes Tom smile. "She'll be a good mum, though."

"She will; better than she realises. And you'll be such a good uncle."

"I hope so. It's nice, isn't it? Even if she's going to be a single mum."

"It is nice. Really nice. There's something about a baby, you know. They might seem boring, and they can't hold a conversation – or anything much at all to start off with – but the life they bring into a family–" Graham's eyes light up at the thought of being a grandad – "I just wish your mum…"

"I know, Dad. I know. She'd have loved it."

"She would."

They watch *Countdown* together, and then Graham wanders off to see to the bird-feeders. Tom looks at the envelope and picks it up.

Carefully, he slides his finger under the glued-down flap, and pulls it open, revealing the back of a card. He takes it out of the envelope. He almost doesn't want to read whatever Cecily has to say, but he's come this far.

Dear Tom,

I hope that you're recovering OK and feeling much better now.

I've been doing a lot of thinking and I realise you were right, it's too soon for you to be getting into a relationship, and that you and your family need each other. That must be your priority. I hope all goes well with Annie's pregnancy. You will be an amazing uncle, I know it.

I don't want to overstep the mark, but I have some details of support organisations, from work, and I thought I'd share them with you. If they are not for you, maybe they'll be of interest to Graham or Kitty and Annie. But it's worth thinking about, Tom. Talking to somebody you don't know

*means you can be as open as you like, and don't risk hurting
anybody's feelings.*

*Anyway, feel free to just ignore that if you'd prefer. I
really just wanted to send you this card because I saw it and
I thought of you. And I wanted to wish you well and say
that I hope we will see each other again one day.*

Love, C xx

Tom unfolds the neat piece of paper, with Cecily's
careful handwriting listing a few different charities
and local bereavement counsellors and groups. He
puts it to one side, and turns the card over. On the
front is a picture of a short-eared owl.

26

Fittingly, Tom's birthday swings around on the weekend that the clocks spring forward. It's been a long, hard winter, and a wet one, too, but for the last week the sun has been on the offensive, creating pockets of warmth if you know where to look.

Here at the long barrow, the light has been flooding the first chamber, and the butterflies which have overwintered here have begun to wake. Likewise, the first leaves on the trees have shyly begun to open, so that the dark, twisted branches of the oak have begun to take on a lightness, as though soaking up the sun's rays.

It's been only a couple of fistfuls of days since Kitty's birthday, and Tom's accident, but there has been so much change.

As the flowers have begun to bloom and lift their faces to the sun, Graham has lifted his head, and taken in more and more of the world around him. Still heartbroken, still bereft, but no longer as inward-looking as before. He does not spend every waking moment feeling as though he is living through a nightmare.

And Annie – my Annie – is just into her second trimester and suddenly she is starting to show. In fact, as soon as that bump began to make itself visible, it's been like there is no stopping it. With it comes a softness, not just around her belly, but in her face. She looks more like Kitty, in fact, than Kitty herself has recently – the drama of recent events having taken their toll on my younger daughter's appetite.

Conversely, despite everything, Annie has never felt so good. Once she broke the news at work, she found women who had previously not really spoken to her (because she intimidated them) warmed up, finding something in common at last. And she returns home to an empty house each night, which actually suits her. She values her space, and this daily chance to reset, and recharge her batteries. Now, although she is still nervous about what's to come, she's taking great pleasure in the developments inside her and cannot wait until she can feel her baby kick for the first time. Already, there has been a strange kind of fizzing sensation, which may have been the baby, or may have been indigestion. Whatever it is, she is finding pregnancy suits her, in ways she could never have imagined.

Last weekend there was a gathering at the barrow to celebrate the spring equinox. It was fascinating. Cecily was there, of course, being her usual charming self, only I could see the sadness there too.

Tom, you fool, I thought, not for the first time, but I live (well, not live exactly – but you know what I mean) in hope.

Now, I await my family's arrival with excitement. They are on their way, I know. All on foot – and Alex is with them, Tom having invited him, which was a bit cheeky in a way but as Alex and Annie are on fairly good terms, there's no big drama.

I've seen Kitty looking at Alex as well, and wondering what on earth she'd been thinking. I know, of course. She was grieving, and newly single, and looking for comfort. Alex was familiar and steady and reliable, and he was kind to her. In the depths of grief, a little kindness can go a long way. And besides, what happened was not so terrible, not really. On the face of it, yes, a stolen kiss between a sister and a husband is a terrible thing, but it was born out of such sadness and confusion, and perceived rejection.

"Let's just put it all behind us, shall we?" Alex had said quietly to her when they'd hugged, slightly awkwardly, on seeing each other again.

"Yes," she'd smiled. "I think that's best."

And Annie, who was standing by and heard these words, smiled benignly, considering how she suddenly felt maternal to all and sundry, including her sister and her estranged husband. It's not just Annie's body which is transforming; it really seems like she is flourishing, mentally and emotionally. She will never be the most socially at ease person but I think now she realises that is not the be-all and end-all. And at night, hand on stomach, she whispers to her baby, about how she is going to do her best to be a good mum, like hers was. It's in these moments that her grief creeps in under the covers with her, and she often finds herself crying but, Annie being Annie, she puts this down to hormones as much as anything and despite her situation – recently motherless and newly separated – she feels far less alone than she used to.

Now, as my family approach the bend to the barrow, Tom whispers urgently, "Stop!"

"What is it?" asks Graham.

"There," says Tom, pointing to the shade of one of the ancient trees that line the route. "Look."

They follow the line of his finger and they see it, too. A hare. Sitting as still and calm as a millpond.

"Thank god Mavis is on her lead," Tom says, although my beautiful dog is showing no sign of wanting to be anywhere but with her humans.

They wait a while, patiently.

"That sun's warm," says Graham.

"The sun does tend to be fairly hot, Graham," Alex says, making everyone laugh. It makes Alex feel good.

Then, taking its time, the hare lollops off, into the hedgerow, and the group moves on once more.

"I haven't been back here," Tom says to Kitty, falling in step with her.

"Since…?"

"Yes, since Cecily and I…"

"Don't you miss her?"

"I guess so. I don't know. I'm still working things out."

"Is the counselling helping?"

"Yes, it is. But I fell apart last night, thinking about this being my first birthday without Mum."

"She always made them special, didn't she?"

They both think back to the cakes I made, and the photo albums I made them all when they turned eighteen. Now those books are treasured possessions for them all. I'd actually borrowed that idea from Mary who I worked with, as she'd done the same thing for her two sons. Albums packed with pictures from their childhood. Taking them up to their supposed adulthood although really, who is an adult at eighteen? We don't ever stop growing up, I suppose, no matter what age we reach.

We had some good birthdays – parties when they were younger, with Pass the Parcel and Musical Statues, and the classic jelly and ice cream, graduating to roller discos and ice skating and go-karting. I loved having their friends around and the noise of it all, although I was also always happy to put it behind me with a big glass of wine at the end of the day.

Kitty, seizing the moment, continues, "But Tom, just because you're sad, it doesn't mean you can't do something that will make you happy as well. I don't think I've seen you with anyone else the way you were with Cecily."

He looks uncomfortable. Just keeps walking forward.

"I'm sorry, I don't want to interfere. And god knows I'm the last person to be giving advice when it comes to somebody's love life. But really, Tom, it was lovely seeing you two together. It felt like the one good thing that's happened lately. Well, that and Annie's baby of course, but you know what I mean. And it's Cecily, and we only know her because of Mum. And I know any of us would do anything to not have had this happen, and to have Mum with us still, but that's not something we can do. All we can do is move forward.

They are turning the bend to the barrow now.

"You haven't organised for her to be here today, have you?" he turns to her, aghast.

"No!" she laughs. "No, I might be wittering on like an interfering sister, but I'm not that bad!"

He relaxes a little.

"But that's not to guarantee she won't be here. She does work here after all."

"I know, and I don't know if I'm dreading seeing her or if I really want to."

Finally – a little chink of light.

"I guess we'll just have to wait and see."

Graham, Annie and Alex are way ahead of them now, none of them able to just take their time.

As Tom, Mavis and Kitty round the corner, they stop. There on the path in front of them is the hare. It is perfectly still, aside from its twitching nose, and it looks at them, steadily.

Tom clutches the handle of Mavis's lead more tightly but, incredibly, she is just as still as the hare. And after a moment or two, though it feels like much longer, the hare turns and moves off again, into the undergrowth and towards the barrow.

"Bloody hell," says Tom. "That was amazing."

"It really was," says Kitty.

They are both thinking the same thing: *Mum?*

I smile. Thinking how we humans want everything to make sense, and have some kind of meaning, but we often get it wrong. Still, that was a special moment, without a doubt.

As the hare hops past the barrow, the group comes back together. It is always a sombre moment, approaching the doorway, each of them thinking of that first time they came here. Yet today the brightness adds a levity which can't be suppressed for long. And, as Graham pushes the numbers into the lock, Alex offers to stay outside with Mavis. He takes her to one of the benches, where he sits soaked in sunlight and breathes deeply, and slowly, as his new yoga instructor tells him to do. He is spending more and more time in the gym, trying out all the classes and working to make sure he is fit and well for his child, for as long as he possibly can be. It's pretty sweet, really, and even Annie is impressed.

And here they come – my husband first, then Annie, Kitty and Tom. They are walking in age order, which makes me smile.

"Pass me your lighter, Tom," says Graham; revealing that he knows Tom smokes. Tom, surprised, does as he is told, and Graham picks up the candle in front of my niche, lighting it and opening the little stained-glass door.

"Hello love," he says softly, looking at the urn. He knows as well as I do that it isn't me, but I also know it's not really the ashes he is addressing. He is just speaking to me in a place where it seems acceptable. And now, rather than taking my urn out, he places the candle behind the glass, and then he takes a small, soft bag from his pocket.

"Here," he says. "We each need to put one of these in the niche."

"What are they?" Tom asks, as he accepts a smooth stone from Graham.

"Crystals," says my husband, as though it's the most natural thing in the world.

"Crystals?" Kitty says. "Dad, are you turning into a hippy?"

"Maybe I've always been one!" Graham laughs. "Your mum and I had a life before you three, you know."

"I refuse to believe that," says Tom.

"You wait," says Graham. "Annie, when your little one's older, he or she's going to think your life only began when they were born."

Annie just smiles, one hand on her tummy and the other clutching her crystal.

"There's amethyst, rose quartz, onyx and apache tears," Graham says. "I don't know who's got what, it's too dark in here, but it doesn't really matter. We'll put them in here with your mum's ashes. And I hope – I hope – they'll help take care of her, wherever she is." He gulps now, holding back a sob.

Annie puts her hand on his arm and Tom hugs him.

"It's a lovely idea, Dad," says Kitty.

"You go first, Tom. It's your birthday," Graham instructs.

As Tom places his stone beside my urn, the candle light reveals it to be one of the darker crystals.

"That's black onyx," says Graham. "It's meant to help if you're struggling with grief, and give protection against negative spiritual energy. Kitty, you next, love."

As Kitty places her stone next to Tom's, Graham says, "That one's apache tears. It's another one to support you during times of grief and sorrow."

"Thanks, Dad," Kitty says, standing back.

Annie now steps forward and lays her stone on the other side of the urn. It is pink, and rougher than the two darker crystals.

"Rose quartz," says Graham, approvingly. "That one's lovely, Annie. It's for unconditional love, and nourishing the heart."

Annie smiles, though she is not somebody who has

ever considered crystals as anything but a cheap bit of tat you might buy at the seaside.

"So I must have amethyst," Graham continues. "This one's for healing and is meant to be even more powerful when it's combined with the rose quartz and onyx. I'm sure the lady said it's meant to help with spiritual and emotional self-awareness as well."

He looks at the four stones next to my urn, standing sentinel beside it. "There," he says, pleased. He closes the stained-glass door and as he does so, my friends here gather round. I smile at them, somewhat overwhelmed, and they envelop me and my family, who each feel an inexplicable warmth, but none of them wants to mention this to the others, in case they sound mad. It's harder to ignore the sight of the candlelight seeming to expand, filling the niche in a way that seems impossible for the size of the flame.

For a few moments, the full image on the door glows and my children and my husband put their arms around each other, gazing at the image of the happy family and lovely home, and the rays of light radiating from the heart-shaped sun.

My friends in death fade back and away.

"We are lucky indeed," Graham says, shedding a silent tear.

"We are," says Kitty, briefly resting her head on his shoulder.

"Here," he says, pulling four small velvet drawstring bags from his pocket. "Take one of these."

"What are they, Dad?"

"It's the same crystals," he says. "Smaller ones, but one of each, for all of us. Keep them in your pocket, or at your bedside. I know it sounds a bit silly, but I thought it was a way of keeping us all connected – all five of us – wherever we are."

"Oh Dad," says Annie.

"I know, it's stupid."

"It's not!" she says. "I mean... crystals... well, you know what I'm like when it comes to things like that, but they're beautiful stones regardless. And I like... I love... the thought that you've done this."

"Yes, thank you Dad, it's lovely." Kitty kisses him on the cheek.

"You old hippy!" Tom grins, and Graham pretends to cuff him round the ear.

"Happy birthday, son."

"Thanks, Dad."

And they sit now on the stone seats, bowing their heads and lost in their own thoughts, but each clutching a small black velvet bag.

In time, they make their way outside, individually. Annie first, walking across to Alex and Mavis. She sits at the other end of the bench to her husband, but she smiles at him.

"Alright?" he asks.

"I think so."

Next comes Kitty, and it's a bit awkward for a moment, just the three of them, and thankfully Tom emerges shortly afterwards. Graham stays on and now he is alone he lets the tears come truly. But he is learning to control them now, these tears, like turning a tap on and off.

"Are those crystals a stupid idea, love?" he asks me, and I try to make the flame on the candle flicker, to some success.

"Is that a yes or a no?" he laughs, though he doesn't really believe it's me making that happen.

I love them, though, and it's like being given a present, even though I'm dead. What a wonderful thing!

When he eventually stands up, thinking he will need to get back and have a shower and get changed before they go out to the Italian restaurant tonight, Graham gazes at the niche door again.

"Lucky indeed," he murmurs, passing his fingers across the five figures there, resting them lightly on the mother figure. "How I miss you."

He opens the door, and he blows out the candle, stepping through the sudden darkness of the chamber and out into the light.

Beginning Again

As they make their way along the path, winding its way back around the barrow, they see her.

Kitty actually spots her car first, pulled up in the parking spot just around the bend. Her step falters for a moment, making Tom look up.

"Oh," he says.

"Erm…"

"It's OK. It's fine."

It's worse for Cecily, thinks Kitty, seeing the whole family group coming towards her. Even Alex who, for all Cecily knew, had been cast outside.

Graham greets her warmly, though. "Hello stranger! How are you?"

"Oh, I'm OK, thank you! I'm just coming to make sure everything's in order for the open day tomorrow." Because, of course, this doesn't stop with me. Always, there are more people coming to see the barrow. Ill people, their families, their friends. People just thinking ahead, or even just curious. Even since my ashes have been placed here, there have been others who have joined us. And Cecily has been here for all of them, supporting them when they want it, or just staying close by.

Annie and Alex say hello but carry on walking, Annie glancing back to see what Tom does. Kitty stops and hugs her, not knowing what else to do, while Tom stands back, his hands clasping each other.

"Hi," he says, as Kitty links her arm in Graham's and moves him on.

"Hello," says Cecily, and she crouches to greet Mavis, who is overjoyed to see her.

"How are you?" Tom asks stiffly.

Come on, I think, *you can do better than that!*

"I'm alright," she says. "It's your birthday, isn't it?"

"It is."

"I'm sorry, I wasn't trying to stalk you. Quite the opposite in fact, I was trying to work out when you'd be here, and come later."

"I'm not surprised you want to avoid me," Tom looks at her.

"No!" she exclaims. "I mean, I didn't want to intrude. But I do have to go and check all the candles are there, and make sure the gravel looks nice. Which sounds ridiculous!" She smiles now.

"Absolutely, got to get that gravel in shape," grins Tom. "Not a stone out of place."

"Want a hand?" he asks.

"What? No, you're just leaving, aren't you?"

"It's fine," he says. "It's my birthday, I can do what I want."

"If you're sure…" She would like nothing more than for him to come with her.

"Of course. Kitty!" he calls, and Kitty turns. "Can you take Mavis? I'm just going to help Cecily."

"What about the meal?" Graham says, and Kitty squeezes his arm.

"It'll be fine, Dad. Let him go."

"You're meant to be going out?" Cecily says. "Don't let me ruin your plans."

"You're not," says Tom. "There's plenty of time."

"Alright."

Kitty jogs up and takes Mavis. "See you in a bit," she says, smiling at them both.

Cecily opens her car boot, taking out a rake and a box of fresh votive candles. Tom finds he wants to unwrap one, and breathe in the fresh, clean smell of the immaculate wax.

He takes the rake from her then he and Cecily turn and walk the path back to the long barrow, and I am brimming with excitement because I know what this could mean.

"What can I do?" asks Tom.

"You sort the gravel out here, and I'll go and check on the candles, and make sure everything's looking good for tomorrow."

"No problem."

Tom hums to himself as he pulls the rake through the stones, finding it strangely therapeutic. He thinks of the small bag of crystals in his pocket, and finds he wants to tell Cecily about them. He begins to pull the rake round in a spiral design, subconsciously mimicking the concentric chamber ceilings.

"That looks amazing!" Cecily says, and he turns, blushing, to see she's been watching him.

"Oh, thanks."

"I might have to ask you to do this every open day."

"No problem!"

"So are you feeling better?" she asks.

"Oh, yeah. I mean, I'm going to counselling. I should have thanked you, for your advice, and for the card."

"Thank you for the owl," she smiles, and he remembers, and grins.

"What an idiot I am."

"Well, I didn't like to say…"

"No, really, I've been so stupid. Honestly, Cecily, I've missed you and I haven't known how to tell you, or even if you'd want me to."

"Shh," she says. "It's OK. Look, have you got a few minutes, or do you need to get back? I really don't want you to miss your birthday meal."

"It'll be fine. Honestly. What are you thinking?"

"Come with me!"

He follows her, and realises where they're going. Back to the field where they'd gone on New Year's Day. It looks so different now; where once it had been bleak, already there are flowers and grasses reaching up towards the sky.

"Hang on," she lays a hand on his arm, and he sees

it: an owl – maybe even the same one they saw before – gliding a long, clean line across the top of the field.

"I think that's the male," she says. "I think they might be a nesting pair, they might even have babies."

"No way."

"He's definitely taking food back somewhere, and then he comes back out again. He's got to be feeding his family."

They stand and they watch, as the owl flies so slowly it doesn't seem possible, the occasional beat of its wings to keep it moving. It turns towards them and Tom sees its round white face and huge eyes. Then suddenly, it swoops and rises again.

"It's got something," Cecily says and, sure enough, there is a tiny body with a long tail clutched in the owl's talons.

"Bad luck, mouse," says Tom.

"I know. It's sad, really. But that owl's a beauty."

The bird disappears from view and suddenly it is just the two of them again.

"Well," Tom says awkwardly, "I suppose I'd better get going."

"I can give you a lift if you like," Cecily says. "Give me a moment to lock up."

"Are you sure?"

"Of course."

They walk back side by side, each so aware of the other's bare arm next to theirs.

"Did you want to say bye? To Ruth I mean," says

Cecily as they reach the barrow, and she feels suddenly foolish.

"I won't," says Tom. "Thank you. I've already been in today."

He stands and waits, looking along the length of the amphitheatre as Cecily locks up. The passing clouds are reflected in the water which flanks the walkway, and small birds flit amongst the reeds.

What a wonderful world, he thinks, remembering listening to that song with me once, and how I'd found myself moved to tears, and he'd teased me about it. Now, he thinks, he feels the same.

"Ready?" he hears Cecily's voice and he turns to her.

"Ready as I'll ever be. Don't mess up my gravel!"

"I'll try not to."

The two of them tiptoe, giggling, around the outer circle of the stones. Tom says, "Come with us. Tonight I mean. If you haven't got anything else planned."

"Really? Are you sure? What about your family?"

"Yes," he beams. "Of course I'm sure. I'd love it if you did and I am quite sure my family will too."

"Then yes please," she says. "I'd love to."

They walk towards her car, and he takes her hand. It is soft, and warm, and familiar. She turns to look at him, her face open and smiling. How could he have let her go before? He smiles back, gently stops her and takes her other hand in his. Then he leans forward and in the warmth of the spring sunshine he kisses her.

"Let's begin again, shall we?"

Acknowledgements

As always, I start this wondering what I have to say of interest! The best place to start is always with the thankyous so let's begin there…

Catherine Clarke, who is a fantastic friend, pickleball partner, cover creator and so much more. I hope you know how much I appreciate you - as do all the Smiths, including the dogs!

My crew of beta readers, who are always so supportive and encouraging, and who offer extremely valuable feedback. Thanks this time to Tracey Shaw, Rebecca Leech, Jean Crowe, Sandra Francis, Ginnie Ebbrell, Amanda Tudor, Roz Osborn, Kate Jenkins, Mandy Chowney-Andrews, Alison Lassey, Hilary Kerr and Denise Armstrong (and sorry for Ash barking at lovely Reggie).

Thanks as always to my dad, Ted Rogers, to whom this book is dedicated. I hope you know how important you are in our lives, and how much I appreciate your help with my books, and your spreading the word about them!

I am very grateful to and for all my family - my mum, dad and two brothers. I realise more and more how lucky we were and are and were to have each other and to get on so well – and now I have my husband Chris and children, Laura and Edward. It's very easy to get caught up in the daily grind of life and, without wishing to sound sanctimonious, it's very good to stop sometimes and remember how fortunate we are. I should also mention here my wider family, from my nieces, nephews, in-laws, aunts and uncles to my cousins, all of whom I love to bits, including my cousin (and friend) Ruth. I did mention to her that I have named a character Ruth, but that she is dead. Thankfully, she didn't seem to mind. I love our swims and chats and cobbled-together picnics. They are a definite highlight and I'm so chuffed we have the chance to spend this time together.

And last, but absolutely not least, my friends. Some friends come and go, but others are definitely for keeps. I've moved around a bit and collected some irreplaceable friends along the way. From my school days and teenage years, uni, work, parenthood and even through my books. I can't say enough how important my friends are in my life and I hope that sometimes some of you see little glimpses of yourselves in my words.

Now a little about the book. As I have mentioned more than once, it's difficult to leave Alice and Julie and Sam and Luke behind in Cornwall. I suspect I will never stop thinking about them and wondering what possible ways their lives have gone! But in this new family I hope I've found some characters who readers will become equally attached to.

It's definitely interesting writing from the point of view of somebody who is dead, and I've enjoyed imagining a possible afterlife. It is an opportunity for a mother to find out so much more about her children's lives than she might have done, and see so many sides of the same story. Clearly my mum's death has influenced me in many ways and has formed a vital part of the inspiration behind this series. It's also left me feeling very strongly that we need to be open about and accepting of death.

I once worked on a wonderful book by New Zealand author and artist Jan Pryor, centred around the death of her son Alexander at the age of four months. A number of things from that book (*After Alexander*) have stayed with me, not least the idea that people stay alive for as long as they are remembered (Jan puts it much better but hopefully you know what I mean). Soulton Long Barrow has provided the perfect inspiration as a place for Ruth and her friends in death to retreat to, and a wonderful, peaceful place for their friends and family to visit. There is space there, and time, and I would wish that for everyone.

I hope that you've enjoyed this book and will go on to enjoy the rest of this series. Who knows what will come next?

FIRST CHRISTMAS

A novella, and the prelude to the

What Comes Next series

This short, festive story is an exploration of another side of this time of year normally packed with family, friends and festivities. It is nevertheless uplifting and engaging, and full of Christmas spirit.

Coming Back to Cornwall

Books One to Ten

Available in print and on Kindle

The whole Coming Back to Cornwall series is being made into audiobooks so you that you can listen to the adventures of Alice, Julie and Sam while you drive, cook, clean, go to sleep... whatever, wherever!

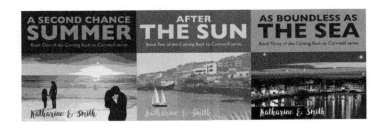

Books One to Five are available now

Connections

Books One to Three

Available in print and on Kindle

Writing the Town Read - Katharine's first novel. "I seriously couldn't put it down and would recommend it to anyone who doesn't like chick lit, but wants a great story."

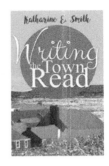

Looking Past - a story of motherhood, and growing up without a mother. "Despite the tough topic the book is full of love, friendships and humour. Katharine Smith cleverly balances emotional storylines with strong characters and witty dialogue, making this a surprisingly happy book to read."

Amongst Friends - a back-to-front tale of friendship and family, set in Bristol.

"An interesting, well written book, set in Bristol which is lovingly described, and with excellent characterisation. Very enjoyable."

Printed in Great Britain
by Amazon

49737083R00169